How to Build and Manage an

Estates Practice

by Daniel B. Evans

LAW PRACTICE MANAGEMENT SECTION
SECTION OF REAL PROPERTY, PROBATE AND TRUST LAW

Commitment to Quality: The Law Practice Management Section is committed to quality in our publications. Our authors and editors are experienced practitioners in their fields. Prior to publication, the contents of all our books are rigorously reviewed by the LPM Publishing Board and outside experts to ensure the highest quality product and presentation. Because we are committed to serving our readers' needs, we welcome your feedback on how we can improve future editions of this book. We invite you to fill out and return the comment card at the back of this book.

Cover design by Gail Patejunas.

Library of Congress Catalog Card Number 99-73037
ISBN 1-57073-718-5

10 09 08 07 06   5 4 3 2

Discounts are available for books ordered in bulk. Special consideration is given to state bars, CLE programs, and other bar-related organizations. Inquire at Book Publishing, American Bar Association, 750 N. Lake Shore Drive, Chicago, Illinois 60611.

Contents

CHAPTER 1
Defining Your Practice   1

CHAPTER 2
Finding Clients 17

CHAPTER 3
Ethics Issues 37

CHAPTER 4
Fees and Fee Agreements   55

CHAPTER 5
Communicating with Clients   73

CHAPTER 6
Managing Files and Information   101

CHAPTER 7
Getting the Work Done   119

CHAPTER 8
Personnel   147

About the Author

Daniel B. Evans received his J.D. cum laude from the University of Pennsylvania and practices law in Wyndmoor, Pennsylvania, mainly in the areas of estate planning, estate and trust administration, and related tax planning for closely held businesses. He also serves as a consultant to Leimberg & LeClair, Inc., Bryn Mawr, Pennsylvania, to develop and improve software for lawyers and estate planners.

Dan is active in the American, Pennsylvania, and Philadelphia Bar Associations, and has written and spoken extensively on estate planning and legal technology. As a member of the ABA Section of Law Practice Management, Dan serves on (among other things) the Editorial Board and as Articles Editor for *Law Practice Management* magazine. He also is currently serving as the "Probate-Technology" Editor of *Probate and Property* magazine, published by the ABA Section of Real Property, Probate and Trust Law, and is a member of the Office Technology Committee of the Probate Section of the Philadelphia Bar.

He is the author of *Wills, Trusts, and Technology: An Estate Lawyer's Guide to Automation,* published jointly by the Real Property, Probate and Trust Law Section and the Law Practice Management Section of the ABA, and is a co-author of *The New Book of Trusts,* published by Leimberg Associates, Inc.

His complete resume, and many of his writings, can be found on the Internet at **http://evans-legal.com/dan**.

Acknowledgments

I would like to thank the Publishing Board of the ABA's Law Practice Management Section for inviting me to write this book, which was a surprisingly interesting experience for me. I would also like to thank Edward R. Parker, K. William Gibson, Sean Flynn, Terry Good, Stephan R. Leimberg, and Richard N. Feferman for their review of my manuscript and their most helpful suggestions, and Beverly Loder for her support and guidance. Special thanks to Edward R. Parker for allowing us to reprint one of his forms as Appendix E.

And I am grateful to my wife, Storm, and my children, Merritt and Griffin, for listening politely and patiently to me as I babble at home about estate practice management and technology, and for giving me the uninterrupted time I needed to write this book.

Preface

A relatively recent development in the world of art is the emergence of the "performance artist," who uses the movements or appearance of his or her body as a kind of canvas of artistic expression. Franz Kafka (1883–1924) may have earlier described a performance artist in *Ein Hüngerkunstler (A Hunger Artist),* a short story about a man who earns a living by performing feats of fasting.

I had a similar sense of *avant garde* when I left a partnership in a large law firm in 1991 to become a solo practitioner. I had been an associate in a small firm (3 to 4 lawyers), an associate in a medium-size firm (20 to 30 lawyers), and an associate and partner in a large firm (120 lawyers). I had different experiences in different firm settings, but I had always been working for someone else. Even as a partner in a large firm, the practice management and marketing decisions affecting my practice had all been made for me. In 1991, thirteen years out of law school, I wanted to start making decisions for myself.

By 1991, I had also been active in the American Bar Association Law Practice Management Section for several years. I had been reading, writing, hearing, and talking about law office technology, value billing, and practice management. Because of the policies and attitudes within my firm, however, I could not actually carry out the ideas about which I had been reading, writing, and talking. I decided it was time to "put my money where my mouth was" and start living the practice I had talked about. It was time to use my own life and practice as a laboratory to test the ideas in which I believed. So I took a deep breath, held my nose, and jumped feet first into the deep and cold waters of a solo practice.

Has it been successful? Eight years later, I'm not rich, but I'm still alive and still working, which is worth something. Moreover, it's been fun, so much fun that I really can't imagine having done it any other way.

I can't give a testimonial that says that if you follow the advice in this book, you will be rich, famous, and irresistible to the opposite sex. However, I believe that if you read this book and think about how to apply some of the ideas to your own practice, your practice—and therefore your life—will be more interesting and ultimately more rewarding.

Which is what it's really all about.

Introduction

Consider this to be a book of ideas.

Like other professions and service-oriented occupations, the practice of law is a form of personal expression. Different lawyers have different styles in the courtroom, in negotiations, and in dealings with clients. Each different style can be successful.

Okay, you might say, the practice of law can conform to personal styles, but what about the management of a law practice? Aren't there rules and standards there? No, not really. Different managers have different styles and different ways to be effective. Some managers can lead by example, without ever seeming to give a direct command. Others are cast in the military mold, and they need to organize and review the troops and issue marching orders to them.

Consequently, this book can't tell you the exact way to build and manage your practice because the best way to build and manage *your* practice ultimately depends on who *you* are. This book can only give you some ideas about things that you might want to try and that might work for you.

Some Comments on the Book's Organization

This book follows the general outline of the Law Practice Management Section's "How to Build and Manage a Practice" series to a large degree. I have, however, made a number of additions, deletions, and other variations to suit the nature of an estates practice, as well as my own predilections.

You should find that the book proceeds in a fairly logical order, from deciding what kinds of clients you want, to finding those clients, to choosing clients and establishing fee agreements, to doing the actual legal work. Not everything can be neatly compartmentalized, and you will find some overlap and some subjects that you may consider miscategorized or otherwise out of place. Nonetheless, you should still find reading the book worthwhile.

Limitations on Scope

There are some subjects and areas that you will not find in this book. This book has not attempted to mimic or recreate the classic book on starting a law practice, Jay G Foonberg's *How to Start and Build a Law Practice,* published by the Law Practice Management Section. There are many general ideas and words of wisdom in that book that are not duplicated here, including a lot of tips and information about how to start a practice. This book assumes that there already is a practice of some sort and the goal is to make it better.

This book deals with some of the impact of technology in building and managing an estates practice, but it does not attempt to analyze the entire range of software available for an estates practice or describe how to choose the most appropriate packages. Those subjects have already been covered (and fairly well, if I say so myself) in my first book, *Wills, Trusts, and Technology: An Estate Lawyer's Guide to Automation,* published jointly by the Real Property, Probate and Trust Law Section and the Law Practice Management Section of the ABA.

Defining Your Practice

1

aim, n. The task we set our wishes to.
—Ambrose Bierce, *The Devil's Dictionary*

ALTHOUGH AN ESTATES PRACTICE might seem to be a rather narrow area of practice, it is possible to develop an even narrower practice within the estates and trusts field. Why, and how, should you do so?

Why Define Your Practice?

Defining your practice might initially strike you as a self-imposed limitation. Why limit the kinds of clients to represent or matters to undertake? Why tie your own hands and limit your practice's growth? The answer is that a narrow practice definition is not intended to limit a practice but, instead, to focus it. There are several good reasons for this strategy.

Competence and Expertise

A primary practical (and ethical) consideration is that it may be too difficult to be knowledgeable and competent in all areas of estate planning and estate administration. For example, one lawyer (or even one estate department or firm) is not likely to be proficient at both generation-skipping tax planning and probate court litigation in will contests. Narrowing your practice to those areas in which you are competent is a practical reaction to the reality that everyone has limitations

Moreover, competence has a cost. It takes time and effort (and therefore money) to develop the technical expertise and practical experience to provide competent representation. Going into a new estate planning technique or area of practice for a single client may simply be too expensive for you and the client. For example, if you have never prepared a family limited partnership, the time and research necessary to become familiar with all the income tax, estate tax, valuation, and related drafting issues may cost too much for one client to pay for one transaction, so it simply would not be profitable to learn the technique for just one transaction. There must be an intention to develop a practice area to serve a series of clients to justify the investment needed to develop the relevant expertise.

Name Recognition

You're more likely to be a big fish if the pond is small. In your particular city, county, or region, it may be difficult to become known as the best estates lawyer. It may be much easier to become known as the estates lawyer most knowledgeable about charitable remainder trusts (or family limited partnerships, joint revocable trusts, or another similarly specific estate planning technique). You can distinguish yourself more easily from your competition if you can define the nature of the competition and thereby narrow the field.

Volume and Profitability

It may also be possible to organize your office more efficiently if you handle many cases of a similar nature rather than many cases of different types. For example, if you develop a practice focus on estate planning for young professionals, you can develop a set of questionnaires, form letters, wills, trusts, and other documents well suited to that clientele. Suddenly handling an estate planning problem for an elderly widower may require modifications that take extra time and reduce profitability.

Marketing Concentration

Marketing is usually more effective if efforts are concentrated on a specific target rather than scattered across several areas. While an advertisement seen once might produce some response, an advertisement seen twice might get more than twice that response. This is because people retain information through repetition, so something seen multiple times is more likely to be retained than something seen just once. When the need for a product or service arises, the potential customer or client is more likely to think first of the provider name most often seen or heard.

Defining a practice area that leads to specific marketing efforts may therefore be more effective than having general, unfocused marketing. Suppose, for example, that you want to develop more estate planning business among the owners of closely held businesses. One tactic would be to contact local business groups to see if they are interested in talks on estate planning strategies. If you provide good information to a number of different groups, you might eventually develop a favorable reputation for your estate planning advice within the business community. Diverting time to other types of marketing for other types of practice areas can dilute the impact of your efforts in the business community and make your efforts there less productive.

Ways to Define Your Practice

Once you decide to define your practice, how many different ways can you look at it? In general, it is possible to define a practice in terms of types of clients, types of assets held by clients, and specific areas of law or estate techniques.

Types of Clients

Age or Health

A colleague once told me that the most successful estates lawyers are those who outlive their clients. Under that theory, the most desirable clients are those advanced in years, or in poor health, whose estate planning files are most likely to "mature" into estate administration files. However, even assuming that there was once some truth to the theory, there are several reasons why it is not accurate today.

- First, performing estate planning for a client does not in any way ensure that the client's executors and trustees will retain you to administer the estate or trust. Children, and even surviving spouses, too often have their own advisors and own ideas about how to administer the estate— and those ideas may not include you.
- Second, estate administration is not necessarily more profitable than estate planning. There is too much competition among lawyers, accountants, banks, and other estate administration service providers to assume that an estate administration will result in fees more profitable than the fees for any other legal service.
- Third, people are very mobile nowadays. Even an elderly client may move to a new state or new community, perhaps for family or health reasons, and may seek new counsel nearer the new residence. Preparing an estate plan for an elderly client is thus no guarantee that the same estate plan will still be in force when the client dies.
- Lastly (and most ironically) effective estate planning often eliminates the need for estate administration services. A good estates lawyer frequently does such a good job in planning that when the client's death finally occurs, there is nothing more for the lawyer to do.

Once you stop thinking of estate planning as a prelude to an estate administration and start thinking of it as a profitable practice in its own right, a client's age becomes irrelevant. The emphasis should be on providing valuable services and earning a reasonable fee now, not on whether fees for different services might be earned in the future.

With all of that in mind, there are still reasons why it might be more effective to market estate planning services to a particular age group. Elder law has become a recognized practice area because the elderly often have different legal and financial concerns from those still working and raising children. The elderly are, for example, more concerned with nursing home costs, Medicare and Social Security benefits, and physical or mental disabilities. Younger clients are, in contrast, more often concerned with a surviving spouse's financial security and younger children's college expenses. Developing expertise and skills geared toward specific age groups—and marketing to those groups—can be an effective practice plan.

The health of the client's beneficiaries can also present opportunities for developing practice specialties. Children with unusual physical, emotional, or mental conditions (e.g., Down's syndrome) create special problems in estate planning. For example, should the parents try to maintain the child's eligibility for Medicaid or other government assistance by disinheriting the child or providing only a "special needs" trust? There are difficult decisions involved, and a practitioner with expertise and experience may be able to develop referral sources at institutions and agencies that regularly deal with disabled children and their parents.

Occupation

Devoting a practice to a specific occupation can be beneficial in two key ways.

First, clients in the same occupation or profession frequently have similar estate planning problems, so expertise can be developed in planning techniques most appropriate to those problems. Doctors, for example, often have substantial estates but are cash poor, having expensive homes, substantial retirement accounts, and large amounts of life insurance, but few liquid investments. Many executives in large corporations have similar estates but with the added complications of stock options and nonqualified executive benefits. (For more examples, see the later discussion of different asset types.)

Second, business and professional groups form a good marketing opportunity. Speaking to professional groups about estate planning problems common to the group can be an excellent way to get public exposure and client contacts.

Wealth

We would probably all like to represent the wealthiest clients, but there really aren't enough of them to go around. That being the case, it makes sense to develop legal expertise that may be of interest to the less than very wealthy.

One obvious example is the revocable trust, which is usually marketed to those more concerned with estate administration costs than with tax planning. Another example is the concept of the "disclaimer" trust, which can provide flexibility to those married couples whose estates may or may not require more sophisticated estate planning. (For more information on this technique, see Daniel B. Evans, "The 'Disclaimer' Trust: An Ideal Estate Plan for the Medium-Size Estate," *Probate and Property,* September/October 1987.)

By developing tools and techniques of interest to the middle portion of the wealth scale and promoting those ideas in newsletters and seminars, an estates lawyer can appeal to a broader client base and, with good practice management, develop a profitable and rewarding practice.

Types of Assets
Developing an expertise in certain types of assets can also lead to marketing opportunities.

Life Insurance
Although life insurance might seem to be an easy area in terms of estate planning (just transfer it to an irrevocable trust), many lawyers have developed good practices by holding themselves out as particularly knowledgeable about life insurance and estate planning with life insurance.

Clients with individually purchased policies are not the only possibilities. Clients may have group term insurance, split-dollar arrangements, and buy-sell agreements funded with life insurance that can present a number of different problems and opportunities. In addition, understanding different life insurance products (e.g., term, whole life, universal life, and variable life, to name but a few) and helping clients to select the type of policy and insurance company best suited to their needs can also prove to be valuable skills and services.

One benefit of expertise in life insurance planning comes when life insurance agents see you as an asset in helping the client understand the value of life insurance and how to integrate it into the estate plan. They are then more likely to bring you into estate planning discussions and to introduce you to clients who need help with their life insurance and estate planning. Proficiency in life insurance planning can therefore lead to sources of new business.

Retirement Benefits

Many people have accumulated large accrued benefits—sometimes in the millions of dollars—because of the tax benefits of qualified retirement plans, the resulting popularity of pension, profit sharing, 401K, individual retirement accounts, and other qualified plans, and the time that has elapsed since those kinds of plans became popular. The retirement benefits are subject to both estate tax and income tax, and there are only a limited number of options for dealing with the tax issues during lifetime and at death. Furthermore, the existing options often include technical restrictions and limitations that require a certain amount of expertise to work around and through. So there is a need for competent planning for retirement benefits, and a growing market of people who need it.

As with life insurance, an expertise in retirement benefit planning can lead to sources of new business. If brokers, insurance agents, financial planners, accountants, and others dealing with retirement benefits find that you have knowledge that can benefit their clients, they are more likely to refer those clients to you.

Business Interests

Business owners also have special planning needs. Specific tax opportunities and problems arise under Internal Revenue Code Sections 303, 2057, and 6166. There are also problems of succession of ownership and control, often solved through buy-sell agreements, employment agreements, voting trusts, and similar contractual arrangements.

Furthermore, owners and their businesses usually have other tax planning and legal needs not directly related to estate planning, such as Subchapter S issues, contracts with customers and suppliers, leases for business premises, compliance with government regulations, and other commercial law problems. Such clients may present opportunities for serving the company's general corporate or business needs, a form of cross-marketing if the estates lawyer also has a business practice or is part of a larger firm with a more general practice.

Farms and Farmland

Farmers and owners of farmland have special valuation issues similar to business owners owing to Internal Revenue Code Section 2032A, as well as the other provisions relating to business interests. Undeveloped farmland also creates opportunities for some more esoteric planning techniques, such as qualified conservation easements.

Although developing a practice in farms and farmlands is limited by geographical proximity to such lands, it is a natural practice focus in farming regions.

Other Special Assets

Various other types of assets can cause estate planning and administration problems because of valuation issues, limited marketability, or special tax treatments for the assets. Examples include art, antiques, and other collectibles; copyrights and patents held by artists and inventors; oil and gas leases and other mineral interests; and racehorses or other forms of livestock.

One of the most unusual estate planning specialties is representing the winners of large lottery jackpots, since those winners have instantly acquired large and illiquid estates with special tax planning problems.

Each of these "problem assets" can lead to expertise that can be marketed to interested trade or professional organizations or other planning professionals likely to encounter these kinds of problems.

Estate Techniques

Another approach is to pick a particular estate planning technique, or estate or trust administration problem, and to focus on the type of service to be provided, rather than on the kind of client or asset.

Obvious examples of this approach are the "living trust" mavens, who hold seminars, write articles, and advertise with a single theme—that a living trust is the greatest thing since sliced bread and a cure for everything but warts. Although many practitioners consider the indiscriminate promotion of living trusts to be as respectable and responsible as the indiscriminate promotion of aluminum siding, it must nevertheless be conceded that this approach can provide an effective marketing plan. The reason is that it offers an understandable benefit to the public and it helps to distinguish the lawyer promoting the trust technique from other lawyers.

Other specialties are possible. Some lawyers are experts in generation-skipping tax planning, estate planning for farms or businesses, grantor retained annuity trusts (GRATs), qualified personal residence trusts (QPRTs), and other similar tax planning techniques. It is difficult to think of building a specialty within estate administration, but some lawyers have been able to build reputations in will contests or in opposing banks in fee disputes.

Almost any time you learn about a new planning technique, or delve into a new legal issue, you should consider how you can use that new expertise to attract new clients.

Profitability

Many commentators have suggested that we are currently experiencing the largest intergenerational transfer of wealth in history, as the generation that came of age before and during the Second World War and benefited from the prosperity that followed passes on that accumulated wealth to the "baby boom" generation. For that and other reasons, there is a demand for estate planning services, and a lawyer who knows the law, is efficient, and serves clients well can earn a good living. Yet is there any one type of estates practice that is more profitable than the others?

Are there "hot topics" in which a lawyer can get an edge by being out in front of the crowd? It only takes about an hour of study a day for about six months to become an expert in anything. So the good news is that within a fairly short time you can become an expert in the area of law that is currently the most profitable. The bad news is that every other lawyer can do the same thing, so no area of the law is going to stay profitable for long merely because of a lack of competition. Constant reading and education are needed to stay current on developments in the law, but you're not going to build a career by hopping from one type of practice to another, always trying to anticipate changes in the legal market and the law.

Some techniques and problems will always draw larger fees because of the perceived need for top-quality legal advice. There are, for example, some lawyers who can earn five-figure fees for forming a family limited partnership (currently a hot ticket in estate planning). Yet why? The partnership agreement itself is usually a standard form, with little customization. The difficult issues are in the valuation of the partnership interests, a problem for an independent appraiser, not a lawyer. However, if there are large amounts of money at risk in a transaction that the Internal Revenue Service has publicly announced it will challenge, there is a natural desire to get the best-quality legal advice. The lawyers who are earning the largest fees for these transactions are not "one-trick ponies" who succeed because of special knowledge about a single tax technique. They are well-respected for their knowledge of a broad range of concerns as well as their judgment in navigating difficult legal issues. They have earned this reputation over the years by serving clients well, winning cases, writing articles, and speaking publicly. Changes in laws and reversals in courts will be merely bumps in their careers, not crashes, because they will always have their clients' appreciation, other lawyers' respect, and their own practice skills.

Ultimately, the lawyers who are able to charge a premium for their services are the lawyers who are able to distinguish themselves from other practitioners in the same field. How do you distinguish yourself?

- ◆ Through the image you create in your marketing (discussed in Chapter 2)
- ◆ Through avoiding conflicts of interest and other ethical problems (discussed in Chapter 3)
- ◆ Through the quality of your communications with your clients (discussed in Chapter 5)
- ◆ Through the perceived quality of your legal services to your clients (discussed in Chapter 7)

Trying to find the area of law or clientele that is currently "hot" or earns the biggest fees is a little like trading for short-term gains in the stock market. You might get lucky and find a company that, with a new technology or a change in market conditions, becomes a quick winner—but you're more likely to guess wrong and lose money. The wealthiest investors are usually investing for the long run, holding on to stocks in companies that they believe will continue to perform well through sound management and proven leadership regardless of future changes in technologies or the economy. You should invest in your career in the same way. You can try to find the right "hot" specialty and make a quick short-term profit, but laws change and clients change, and what is most profitable today will not necessarily be so tomorrow. If, however, you invest your time in creating a long-term career by working in an area of the law that you enjoy and spending the time needed to improve your knowledge of the law, practice management skills, and client relationships, you will be profitable and successful.

Types of Firms or Offices

Another practice decision is the type of firm or office to build. Large law firms have a different appeal from small or medium firms or solo practices. An estates department within a larger general practice firm may have different objectives from a boutique firm that specializes in estates work.

Estates Departments

Building an estates department within a larger firm can present some interesting challenges.

One challenge is that an estates department may be viewed as a service to other clients of the firm rather than as an important, profitable practice in its own right. The estates department may be seen as a "loss leader" that allows the firm to hold itself out as a full-service firm and to prevent certain clients from going elsewhere. In essence, it is not part of the firm's larger vision. As a former partner of mine caustically observed, a corporate partner who has just completed a multimillion-dollar closing for a client, thereby earning a six-figure fee for the firm, might invite the client to "pick up a will on the way out."

Policies within the firm that are appropriate for other departments may also create obstacles for an estates department. A firm that insists on hourly billing may not be able to understand or accommodate an estates department that wants to adopt fixed-fee billings for estate planning and administration.

Building an estates department within a larger firm therefore requires that the responsible partners develop a vision and plan for the department that allows the department to serve the firm's clients while also creating a reputation and practice for the department that contributes to the firm's image and profitability.

Small and Boutique Firms

An estates practitioner in a smaller firm will have more influence over the firm's marketing decisions, but there will still be other decisions to be made and other lawyers with whom to coordinate.

In a boutique firm limited to estates practice, different lawyers can follow different specialties. (Indeed, it adds to the firm's strength to have expertise in different areas.) The firm should still have a special focus, however, to distinguish itself from other estate firms and to provide a focus for the firm's marketing efforts.

An estates lawyer in partnership with lawyers from other practice areas will face problems similar to the estates department in a large firm. The partnership will not make economic sense without cross-marketing, which means that the estates lawyer should be able to serve the needs of the firm's other clients and attract clients who will also be interested in the firm's other services. As in a larger firm, the estates lawyer's focus should serve and complement the focus of the entire firm.

Solo Practitioners

In a group practice, the lawyers' different experiences and abilities can be combined to serve the clients' needs. Without partners or associates to draw on, solo practitioners are limited by their own expertise. This means that a solo practitioner may need to limit his or her own practice to a greater extent than lawyers practicing in a group. However, a solo practitioner has greater freedom to make individual practice decisions, without worrying about how it will affect nonexistent partners.

Home Offices

A home office probably represents the smallest possible firm. There are typically few, if any, personnel other than the practicing lawyer and little of a law firm's usual appearance. Clients will therefore perceive a lawyer based out of a home office differently from a lawyer with a larger (and more expensive) downtown office. These differences can be an advantage to the lawyer with a home office, depending on the type of clients and practice the lawyer is trying to attract.

Many clients may prefer to deal with a lawyer working out of the home, considering the lawyer to be more economical, convenient, or compatible with the client's attitudes and lifestyle. Some clients, though, may consider a home office to be unstable or transitory.

Some people may feel more comfortable with an individual lawyer in a local office than with a large firm with offices downtown or in another part of the area. On the other hand, an executive or business owner may feel less comfortable dealing with a single lawyer in a home office.

Younger clients may not be as wedded to the common notions of what a lawyer is supposed to look like, and what kind of office a lawyer is supposed to have, and so will be more willing to try a lawyer with a different way of practicing. At the same time, older clients may be more interested in a good personal relationship with their lawyer and so more willing to work with a lawyer they trust, regardless of the office arrangements.

A suburban location can be an advantage in attracting suburban residents but a disadvantage in attracting urban residents and businesses.

Taking all those factors into account, an estates practice may be well suited to a home office because it is usually directed to older suburban residents and typically does not require a large staff or multiple associates. Furthermore, most of the work is either meeting with clients (which can be done at their homes) or "office" work such as document drafting, tax return preparation, and accounting. Rarely is it necessary to spend much time in court or to meet with opposing lawyers, witnesses, or other third parties.

However, there ain't no such thing as a free lunch. Running a home office means saving on office rent, but there can be other costs. As previously suggested, many lawyers who work out of their homes are more willing to travel to the client's home or business for client meetings, which can be a convenience to the client and attractive to clients *if the client does not need to pay for the travel time.* The home office therefore represents a tradeoff in which the time spent by the lawyer traveling is the "cost" of not having a regular office. Having a home office also puts the lawyer farther away from law libraries, copy centers, postal and shipping services, and other facilities frequently needed by lawyers and their staffs.

Because of zoning and other residential-use restrictions, a lawyer may be prohibited from having employees in the home, or the number of employees may be severely restricted. This can put a cap on overhead but may further increase the clerical types of tasks on which a lawyer may need to spend time.

To the extent that a home office limits a practice—whether in the types of cases the lawyer may take or types of clients the lawyer might attract—there is a "cost" to the office that must be taken into account.

How to Choose

Given the desirability of defining your practice and the wide range of practice choices, how do you decide what to do?

Some choices will be dictated by who you are. Over time, you will find that the little personal choices you make will have shaped your practice much more effectively than any major business decisions. If you don't like dealing with conflicts, you will not want to specialize in estate litigation. If you have difficulty with mathematics and probabilities, you may not be comfortable explaining the mechanics of GRATs to clients.

Many practice "choices" will be dictated by what opportunities become available to you. For example, it is easier to develop a practice based on the clients you already have than to start from scratch and try to attract a completely different kind of client. If your first clients are college friends with new families and lots of life insurance, you might want to become proficient in estate planning for young professionals with lots of life insurance and think about how to attract other similar clients. If a friend asks if you would like to give a speech to a local entrepreneurs association, you might want to study up on tax and financial planning for start-up companies and small business owners and consider whether that kind of clientele fits into your practice goals. In other words, it is easier to take advantage of opportunities you have than it is to develop opportunities you don't have. A bird in the hand is worth two in the bush, you've got to shoot the ducks while the ducks are flying, and opportunity knocks only once, so you should be talking to potential new clients and not wasting time on hackneyed metaphors.

A final suggestion: Don't be too rigorous about all of this. Opportunities and personal choices may also lead you to broaden or diversify your practice instead of narrowing it. As logical as it may be to have a practice focus, it is natural to look for new challenges and an occasional change of pace. A lawyer concentrating in tax planning might, for example, take on a family conflict over trust investments. As long as the shift is into an area in which the lawyer has (or can develop) the necessary level of competence, and the lawyer exercises due discretion in not going in over his or her head, these kinds of professional diversions can help to keep the practice interesting and enjoyable.

Remember, enjoyable is a worthy practice goal, too.

Finding Clients 2

First, catch a rabbit.

—From a recipe for rabbit stew

YOU CAN'T DO ANY ESTATE PLANNING or estate administering until you have a client. You can't have a client until you've met someone who needs a lawyer. Thus, the first order of business is to meet people who are potential clients.

Friends and Relatives

It is natural to start to look for clients among people you already know. Contacts from your college or law school, church or temple, social clubs, community organizations, and neighborhood groups can be included in marketing efforts, in addition to relatives and friends, if done in good taste and within the bounds of professional ethics. For example, there is no reason not to include people you know on a mailing list for a newsletter or a seminar announcement. It is generally considered to be a form of advertising permitted by Rule 7.2 of the ABA *Model Rules of Professional Conduct*. Most people would not be offended by an offer of free information. On the other hand, a direct personal solicitation of employment (e.g., approaching a friend on the golf course and asking if she has updated her estate plan under the new tax law) could violate both good taste and Rule 7.3 of the *Model Rules.*

While friends and relatives are a natural place to start to look for clients, make sure that you don't stop there. It is a sad comment when lawyers can't tell their friends from their clients. One would like to think that it's possible to have a friend who is just a friend without trying to turn the friend into a client, that it's possible to have a client who is just a client without trying to turn the client into a friend. It was said about an elderly estates lawyer that, when one of his friends died, you didn't know whether to console him on the loss of a friend or congratulate him on the administration of new estate.

Referrals from Clients

One of the best sources of referrals is an existing client who gives your name to a friend, neighbor, relative, or business associate. To get referrals from your clients, however, you have to leap two hurdles.

- ◆ The client must be satisfied. Clients will not stick out their neck and give your name to a friend or business associate unless they genuinely value your services. Being adequate is not enough. The client must believe that your services have been superior, if not outstanding. (For suggestions on client satisfaction, see Chapter 5.)
- ◆ The client must remember you. Once again, it's not enough that the client will give your name when asked. You want a client who is so impressed by who you are and what you do that the client will give your name to a potential client without being asked. The only reason clients will do so is that you are on their mind. That is why newsletters to clients (discussed later in this chapter) can be so valuable— not just so that the client will remember you and return to you, but so that the client will remember you and send someone else to you as well.

Referrals from Other Professionals

One of the best sources of new business is referrals from life insurance agents, accountants, investment advisors, and other professionals who deal with tax and wealth planning. Unfortunately, many lawyers see accountants and financial planners as competition instead of marketing resources, which can be a limiting attitude.

As in other areas of law, there is competition in estate and trust law, both among lawyers and between lawyers and other professionals. Accountants can provide tax advice, prepare tax returns, and do the bookkeeping for estates. Bankers, life insurance agents, and financial planners all provide estate planning advice, and banks also provide estate administration services. In a sense, these other service providers are competitors, and each of them can provide some services of use to clients. It is also possible that they can provide some services more efficiently or economically than some law firms.

However, if these "competitors" are more efficient or economical for some types of services, it means that those services are not as profitable for law firms as other types of services. Thus, these competitors are actually relieving lawyers of less profitable work and allowing lawyers to concentrate on more profitable work. Furthermore, there are still many types of services (e.g., will and trust drafting, complex legal and tax analysis, court proceedings, and dispute resolution) for which lawyers are still needed, even by competitors. Maintaining good relations with other service providers can therefore result in referrals and additional legal work which might otherwise go to other lawyers.

By working *with* various kinds of service providers, not against them, it is possible to build a larger and more profitable practice than you could by competing against them. Following are some examples.

Life Insurance Agents

Selling life insurance often goes hand in hand with estate planning. It is a form of planning for death, and many people think of reviewing their wills and estate planning when they are considering life insurance. Many insurance agents sell life insurance for the purpose of paying death taxes, so death tax projections (and death tax planning) are part of life insurance marketing. For many people, buying life insurance creates an estate tax planning problem (or an opportunity) where none previously existed.

Most life insurance agents are trained in basic estate planning and can talk fairly knowledgeably about the federal estate tax marital deduction, unified credit trusts, annual gifts, and even irrevocable life insurance trusts. They cannot (or at least should not) prepare the wills and trusts needed to carry out the tax planning that they are recommending. A good life insurance agent will educate the clients, develop an estate plan, and then look to a lawyer to carry out and complete the plan. The agents will spend time collecting information, calculating taxes, and discussing alternatives with the clients, after which the lawyer can review the estate plan, confirm the key decisions with the clients, and then earn a fee for efficiently generating the documents and taking care of the details that lawyers are trained to handle. In other words, the life insurance agent can perform all of the time-consuming services that clients often don't appreciate, leaving the lawyer to earn what may be the same fee for the same estate plan that could have been developed without the agent, but spending less time than is ordinarily needed. By working with life insurance agents, a lawyer may be able to perform estate planning services much more efficiently and profitably than by working alone.

Life insurance agents also have a marketing advantage because they are not bound by the same ethical restrictions as lawyers. Agents can advertise, make cold calls, and more actively solicit estate planning clients. A life insurance agent might therefore be able to generate a larger volume of referrals than could a lawyer individually.

Accountants

Some accountants work in estate planning, but it is more common to work with accountants in estate administration, either because the decedent's accountant is one of the executors or because the client or executor is convinced that the accountant can perform routine bookkeeping and tax return preparation services more economically than the lawyer.

The client is sometimes (but not always) right. Allowing a good accounting firm to do the bookkeeping and to prepare the tax returns for an estate is not that much different from using a paralegal to do the same work. Once again, the lawyer can perform the services for which the lawyer is best qualified, taking care of the court filings and legal compliance and reviewing the tax returns prepared by the accountants.

The client is wrong about the economics of using an accountant when the accountant does not really know what he or she is doing. Most accountants are not familiar with fiduciary accounting principles and death tax returns, so the lawyer may have to remain responsible for those areas. The bookkeeping and income tax returns for an estate or trust, however, resemble the bookkeeping and income tax returns for individuals and businesses enough that most accountants can provide adequate service to an estate or trust with minimum guidance from a lawyer.

For a solo or small firm with limited paralegal resources, having an accounting firm perform estate administration services allows the lawyers to earn their fees for their services without the overhead of maintaining a paralegal staff (and without the risk that a court might question the fees attributable to paralegal services).

Financial Planners

Many so-called financial planners are really just life insurance agents with a little more training and a lot less discretion. There are, however, accountants and other service providers who hold themselves out as financial planners who are well qualified to perform the services they advertise.

Lawyers can work effectively with financial planners in the same way that they work with life insurance agents and accountants. The exact nature of the relationship will depend on whether the financial planner is selling products (like a life insurance agent) or services (like an accountant).

Independent Paralegals

Some states now recognize "independent" paralegals, who can perform some quasi-legal services without a lawyer's supervision. Although my state, Pennsylvania, has no rules regarding independent paralegals, I have known of former trust officers and book-keepers who charge fees for performing the bookkeeping, tax returns, and other administrative tasks required for estate administration. Working with these kinds of independent paralegals should not be much different from working with accountants. The independent paralegal can perform the routine, repetitive tasks but needs a lawyer if there are interesting legal or tax issues, court filings, or a dispute with or among beneficiaries. If independent paralegals are allowed by local law, lawyers are better off working with them to improve the quality of services to clients and to cultivate them as a source of referrals for problem estates; rather than competing with these service providers for routine estate administrations.

Advantages of Cooperation

Many lawyers are control freaks who are not satisfied unless they can monopolize all aspects of the planning and administration of a client's estate. Flexibility and the ability to work with others, though, can serve both the lawyer and the client.

The various types of non-lawyer service providers who work in estate planning and administration each have their strengths and weaknesses, their advantages and disadvantages. Learning how to work with these service providers, and how to exploit their strengths, can help lawyers provide better and more economical services to clients, improve the lawyer's profitability, and enlarge the lawyer's practice by creating new referral sources.

Newsletters

Newsletters won't work for every type of practice. For example, newsletters don't seem right for a personal injury or family law practice because you cannot target your mailings to those about to be injured or divorced. Similarly, it is difficult to identify who is likely to have a relative die and need estate administration services. Yet you can target newsletter mailings to those likely to need estate planning services, and you should seriously consider publishing a newsletter as part of any marketing program for an estates practice.

Publishing your own newsletter can have several benefits.

- ◆ Newsletters remind people of who you are. It will be a very big coincidence if you happen to send someone a newsletter just as they realize they need legal services of the type you offer. The goal is to get your name into a prospect's consciousness so that, when the need for your services arises, your name will be the first to spring to mind. This means that you can't send out just one newsletter and expect results. You must send out a series, on a regular basis, to remind people of who you are and what you do (and maybe also suggest how you are more qualified than other lawyers).

- ◆ Newsletters can suggest needs that were not previously known. Sometimes people have legal needs that they don't recognize. A person with a large life insurance policy may not know that life insurance is subject to federal estate tax or that the tax can be avoided by transferring the policy to a trust. People concerned about possible disability may not realize that they can avoid costly guardianship proceedings by signing a power of attorney. People who hold assets jointly with one child may not realize that the one child will be the sole owner of the assets at death and will not be required to share the assets with the other children. The list can go on and on. In any event, changes in the law, popular myths, and simple ignorance may lead people to do things incorrectly. A newsletter can help them see the value of seeking legal advice and doing things the right way.

- ◆ Newsletters can generate goodwill by providing information that people appreciate. Even if the prospect doesn't currently need your services, or decides to use another lawyer, he or she may appreciate the information you have provided. That gratitude or goodwill may be helpful in getting business (or maybe a referral) from that prospect in the future.

What to Say in Your Newsletter

A newsletter should provide information that is useful and interesting. There are several different categories of such information.

- ◆ **Basics:** First, there is a great deal of basic information about estate planning and administration that the general public doesn't know but should know, and is often curious about. Why does anyone need a will? What is a durable power of attorney? What happens to minor children upon the deaths of the parents? How long does it take to probate a will? How much does it cost to probate a will? Is life insurance part of the estate? How are retirement benefits taxed? Are the beneficiaries of the estate responsible for the debts if there aren't enough assets? Do nursing homes take all your assets? Will gifts to children save taxes?

- ◆ **Popular topics:** In addition to the basic information, there are hot topics that get reported (and frequently garbled) in the popular press. People are curious about these subjects, and they will be interested in what you have to say about living trusts, family limited partnerships, qualified personal residence trusts, Medicare qualifying trusts, and other subjects mentioned in newspapers and on television.

- ◆ **Changes in the law:** News about changes in relevant laws can provide valuable information as well as impress people with your diligence and timeliness. Relevant laws can include laws and rules relating to wills, trusts, inheritances, joint accounts, and other substantive areas. The most important news, however, usually relates to changes in tax laws because taxes are a concern for most people. You don't need to worry about being the first to announce the new changes, or providing the best explanation, because tax laws are hard for many people to understand and they will read several reports about the same tax law just to ensure that they understand it. In fact, clients might think that your summary was the best of the three they read only because it took three explanations for the new law's meaning to sink in and your explanation happened to be the last one read.

◆ **Selected topics:** Even if it is not a new or popular topic, you can write about a particular tool or technique that might be of interest to clients. You never know what might interest people, so the choice of subjects could be as diverse as charitable lead trusts, deferral of taxes on closely held businesses under Section 6166, different kinds of marital deduction formulas, or use of family settlement agreements to distribute estates without court approval.

◆ **New services:** You might occasionally add a new service or capability to your practice, in which case you should not be bashful about announcing it. This could include new software for tax return preparation, use of e-mail to communicate with clients, or a new tax technique added to your repertory of planning tools.

◆ **Professional news:** Professional news that should be announced includes elections or appointments to professional organizations, new books or articles written, speeches given, and other additions to your professional résumé.

How to Publish a Newsletter

Some bar organizations and publishers sell preprinted newsletters on which you can put your name and address and then distribute them as "yours." This is not recommended for several reasons.

First, it is simply not that difficult to write and print your own newsletter. You only need to fill two to four pages, and it doesn't require law review articles.

Second, a preprinted newsletter is not likely to reflect your particular practice focus. If, for example, you have decided to focus your practice on the needs of the elderly, a newsletter discussing changes in the taxation of closely held businesses but not possible future changes in Social Security and Medicare will not meet your target audience's needs. It is also unlikely that the newsletter will address the special legal news of your state or locality.

Third, a preprinted newsletter is not really going to talk about you. A newsletter should be your opportunity to talk to your clients about your practice, the services you want to provide, and how you intend to provide them. Buying a newsletter means that you are providing something impersonal that has little to do with you or who you are. One size does not fit all. You are better off printing a one-page newsletter that reflects your personal effort than a sending a polished four-page newsletter that could have come from anyone.

Once you decide to create a newsletter, the rest is easy. Any decent word processor can be used to create an acceptable newsletter. (The documentation for the word processing software probably has sample newsletters included as sample documents.) Any printer or copy center can print and fold your newsletter to your specifications.

Building a newsletter distribution list may take some time, but once you have created your initial list, it should be relatively easy to maintain and update it for future mailings. As discussed in Chapter 6, it is strongly recommended that your office adopt a client information or case management system that ensures that names and addresses are constantly updated, so that your mailing list is never out-of-date.

For more information on how to create your own newsletter, see Milton W. Zwicker's *Successful Client Newsletters: The Complete Guide to Creating Powerful Newsletters,* published by the ABA Law Practice Management Section.

Public Speaking

Business associations, retirement groups, churches, and civic organizations may all have an interest in subjects related to estate planning, such as business succession, retirement income planning, and planned giving. Even speeches to professional groups that include other lawyers can provide business opportunities through referrals from lawyers with conflicts of interest or contacts with potential clients to whom you are closer geographically.

If you enjoy public speaking (and many people do not), don't sit back and wait to be invited. Look for business, social, religious, and civic groups in your area that have meetings or might serve as a forum for a speaker. Then get in touch with them. The best contact is through someone you already know within the organization, but if you don't know anyone, you can send a letter to the organization identifying topics on which you are qualified to speak that might interest the organization's members. The worst that can happen is that your letter is ignored, but you might end up speaking to a large group of people interested in your expertise.

When you are invited to speak to a group, remember why you were invited and make sure that you do your best to deliver what you promised. It is not necessary to "sell" your services or impress anyone with your qualifications as an estates lawyer if you deliver the speech that you were invited to give. If you provide the information you promised in an interesting way, you will create your desired impression. Give a few brief examples of how the topic of your speech fits into your own practice. That should be sufficient illustration for your audience to know—and remember—what you do for a living and that you are the best person to go to for help with estate or trust questions.

Seminars

If you are not willing to wait for an audience to invite you to speak, you can write your speech, call it a seminar, and invite an audience to come and listen. Seminars can be used effectively to market an estates practice. They can provide an introduction to new prospects, a service to past or existing clients, and a way to enhance your recognition with the general public. In planning a seminar, keep the following suggestions in mind:

- ◆ Provide a focus. A seminar should have a "hook," something to intrigue people and draw them in. "How to save estate taxes" doesn't quite do it. "Using charitable remainder trusts as private retirement funds" is a little complicated, but it may get more attention than a broader, vaguer title.
- ◆ Share the risks and rewards. Renting a meeting room or other space for a seminar, printing invitations and advertisements, and providing refreshments all cost money. There is a risk that it will be wasted money if not enough people attend. To spread out your risk, try conducting a

seminar in conjunction with a life insurance agent, accountant, bank or trust company, or other professional providing related services. By combining mailing lists, you will broaden your audience and have the opportunity to get new clients from the attendees invited by your cosponsors.

◆ Give the attendees useful information. As in other types of public speaking, you need to deliver what you promise. Although your primary purpose in conducting the seminar is to sell your services, you need to give attendees enough information, enough value for attending, that they believe their time was well spent. Attendees usually understand that a certain amount of time will be spent in self-promotion, and they are willing to accept that time as a cost of attendance. But if no useful, practical information is provided the seminar may generate more bad will than goodwill and will represent money ill spent.

Advertising

Paid advertising in newspapers, magazines, radio, television, or other media is permitted by the *Model Rules of Professional Conduct,* but it is not likely to be effective for an estates practice. Unlike a bankruptcy or personal injury practice, which can draw clients from every walk of life and may need to communicate with people who have never before needed a lawyer, estate planning and administration services are usually delivered to people with above-average incomes and educations. Typically these people either already know a lawyer or have a friend or adviser who knows a lawyer. It seems rather unlikely that a mass media advertisement would attract a person who needs an estates lawyer and who has no other way of finding a lawyer except through an advertisement.

Although paid advertising might not make sense, other forms of "advertising" might be effective. For example, writing a legal or financial advice column for a local newspaper can provide "free" publicity (though it's not really free because you still need to spend the time writing the column). Such a column could well come to the notice of people who might need and want your services.

The Internet and the World Wide Web

A question often asked by lawyers about the Internet is whether you can really get any clients from it. The answer is yes. I know, because I have gotten clients from the Internet, and I can tell you how.

Internet Basics

For those who don't already know, the Internet is a global network of networks that is the closest we now have to an "information superhighway." Although the Internet was originally designed for the government and originally used mainly by colleges and universities, the growth in the general public's use of the Internet has been nothing short of phenomenal over the past few years. Using the Internet, it is now possible to get information from government agencies, private businesses, and a variety of people and places.

This information is usually provided through the World Wide Web, which requires special software called "browsers" to view pictures and documents formatted using Hypertext Markup Language (HTML). While viewing an HTML document using a Web browser, a user can use a computer mouse to click on a word, phrase, title, or picture and immediately cause the browser to display a new part of the document—or an entirely new document from the same or another part of the Internet—that includes new information about the word, phrase, title, or picture. The linking together of different documents across the Internet is why it is called a "web."

One of the more interesting and useful developments on the Internet is the availability of general-purpose "search engines" that can be used to find information of almost any type on the Internet. For example, the Alta Vista search engine **(http://www.altavista .digital.com)** sends out electronic "spiders" or "bots" onto the Web that search for new Web documents, then indexes them so that a user can find any document just by the words used anywhere in the document. Other search engines work in other ways. Another popular search site is Yahoo **(http://www.yahoo.com)**, which attempts to organize Web sites hierarchically and provides some word-searching capabilities.

If a lawyer or law firm publishes information about itself or its practice on the Internet and that information is indexed by a search engine, a potential client looking for legal information or a particular kind of lawyer or firm may be able to find the Web pages of the lawyer or firm through that search engine. At least, that's the theory. In practice, there are some problems, not the least of which is that there are lots of lawyers on the Internet. Running a search for "estates" and "lawyer" will return hundreds of listings.

Who Is Looking

To figure out how to get found on the Internet, you first need to know who is looking and what they're looking for. Based on the responses I have received from my Web pages and the types of clients I have obtained through the Internet, there are two different types of people looking for two different kinds of information about estates.

A significant number of people are on the Internet looking for information about estate planning. These people may not actually be looking for a lawyer but simply doing background research to determine whether they need estate planning or a lawyer. Many are looking for free information, but some may be potential clients and may contact you if your services seem to suit what they perceive to be their needs and you are located close enough to make a consultation feasible.

What I did not expect was the number of inquiries from people living outside of my state who were looking for information on probate procedures in my state, usually because a parent or other relative had died (or was close to dying) in my jurisdiction. Although surprising at first, this now seems very natural. Suppose that you have moved to California but your elderly mother or father were still living in Pennsylvania. If your parent died and you wanted to find information on probate procedures in Pennsylvania, you might very well turn to the Internet for some research. If you found a lawyer who provided some useful information and seemed to be the kind of lawyer you might need, you might get in touch with that lawyer to find out what might need to be done (and how much it might cost) for legal proceedings in Pennsylvania. If a relative has died in Pennsylvania, an out-of-state benefi-ciary (not fiduciary) might want to consult with a lawyer about the proceedings in Pennsylvania and whether the beneficiary's rights are being respected in those proceedings.

Therefore, although there are opportunities to contact clients in your state through the Internet, there are also opportunities to contact out-of-state clients with estate or trust interests in your state. In fact, most of the clients I have gotten through the Internet have been from the second group, not the first. People who need a lawyer in a particular state have limited sources to choose from and might very well go to the Internet to find that lawyer. People looking for a lawyer close to where they live, however, can ask friends, neighbors, relatives, and other local referral sources to help them in their search.

How to Get Found

The three most important factors in real estate are location, loca-tion, and location. The three most important considerations for an Internet Web page are content, content, and content. Getting found on the Internet is more than just putting up a "home page" with a description of your practice, then sitting back and waiting for the clients to roll in. In fact, publishing on the Internet is more like publishing a newsletter than publishing an advertisement. Without interesting and useful content, no one will ever find you— or, even if they find you, they will not remember you.

Providing content helps you to get found in two different ways. The content that you provide can be indexed by Internet search engines, and more specific content increases the chances of being found by a more specific search. For example, a search for the words "estate planning" will turn up thousands of sites, but a search for "California revocable trust with community property" may turn up only a few. The more specific content you provide, the greater your chances of being one of those few.

Providing content also increases the chances of being included in "links" from someone else's Web site. On the Web, pages can provide hypertext links to other pages that enable users to jump from page to page and site to site just by clicking on a link.

Although search engines provide an automated way of finding Web pages, many people provide their own indexes to Web sites, based on their personal judgments about what is useful or valuable. Many people find relevant Web pages by jumping from site to site until they locate what they want. For example, my Web pages include a list of other lawyers in other states who have put together Web pages that I think provide useful information about estate planning or administration in their states. I do this as a service to the people who find my Web pages but really want information on a different state. Some other lawyers in other states have similar links to my Web pages for similar reasons. Providing interesting and useful content on your site increases the chances of being included in a web of estate pages.

What content can you provide? The most valuable information is going to be specific and practical, not general or theoretical. Consider the following suggestions:

- ◆ Estate administration procedures. What seems to be the most popular page on my Web site is a simple list of the tasks required of an executor and when those tasks must be completed. (It is reproduced in this book as Appendix H.) This would seem to be too easy and obvious, but for someone facing an estate administration who has no idea of what to do, a simple checklist or timetable can be extremely valuable and reassuring.

- ◆ Local probate procedures. How do you probate a will? What forms need to be filed, and where are they filed? Do the witnesses to the will need to appear? Who else needs to appear? How long does it take, and what does it cost? What notices need to be sent, and to whom? Once again, these are the simple questions that bother people who have never had to deal with an estate.

- ◆ Death taxes. Most estates lawyers will write about the federal estate tax, but what about state inheritance tax? Is there one? How is it calculated? When is it due?

- ◆ Other probate costs. In addition to filing fees and taxes, other common concerns include executor's commissions and legal fees. If there are official (or unofficial) appraiser's fees or other costs to be considered, that information will be valuable to potential clients.

◆ Will and trust basics. Potential estate planning clients will likely be interested in knowing what normally goes into a will or revocable trust, the formalities of executing a will or trust, and the mechanics of funding and administering a revocable trust. Any information that you can provide specific to your state should be especially valuable.

◆ Estate planning strategies. Information about common estate planning strategies (using the unified credit and marital deduction, irrevocable life insurance trusts, etc.) will appeal to people looking for general estate planning information or an estate planning lawyer.

◆ Asset protection strategies. Another topic that draws a significant number of responses is information on strategies to protect assets from possible future creditors, medical expenses, professional malpractice exposure, business reversals, and so forth. Much of this information is state specific, involving issues such as the rights of creditors in jointly owned property, life insurance, annuities, and self-settled trusts. It therefore represents another opportunity to distinguish your Web pages from the pages of other lawyers in other states.

◆ Powers of attorney and living wills. Other popular topics include the use of durable powers of attorney and the problems relating to medical decisions, either by the family or through advance health care declarations ("living wills"). If your state has a statutory form of either a power of attorney or a living will, you might consider publishing the form on your Web page. You probably would not have earned much of a fee from completing a simple form, but people who want to see the form might have other, more profitable estate planning needs. You might also benefit from favorable publicity and word of mouth.

◆ Newsletter articles. Any other articles that have been published in your newsletter, or are suitable for publication in a newsletter, are also suitable for a Web page.

How to Publish

The mechanics of setting up Web pages are not particularly challenging. Indeed, most word processors can automatically convert word processing documents to HTML documents suitable for publishing on the Internet. A variety of inexpensive Web authoring tools also are available from software publishers (and over the Internet itself). Even HTML coding by hand is not that difficult to understand. (I taught myself how to code HTML documents and converted four years of my newsletters onto a Web site in one weekend, using nothing but a word processor and information that I found on the Internet on how to create HTML "tags.") For detailed information on how to design and construct Web pages, see Kenneth E. Johnson, *The Lawyer's Guide to Creating Web Pages,* published by the ABA Law Practice Management Section.

Although the mechanics of Web authoring are best left to others, I still have some ideas to emphasize. First, every page should use all the words for which your potential clients are likely to search. If one of your goals is to attract clients interested in Illinois probate procedures, every page should have the words "Illinois probate" somewhere on it. If, for example, you write an item on revocable trusts or the taxation of joint property, you should still mention how those planning techniques are affected by Illinois probate laws. Another way to accomplish the same thing is through HTML "meta" tags, which the user does not see while viewing the Web page but which allow you to specify the keywords to be used by search engines to index the Web page. (However, some search engines are suspicious of those kinds of hidden words and have begun to ignore or discount them. Those kinds of hidden words are sometimes used to boost the "relevance ratings" of Web pages to get those pages placed higher in the list of documents returned to the user by the search engine.)

Second, every page should have your name and address on it and should link back to your home page. It is amazing how many Web pages have no references to the author. You are creating these Web pages as advertising, so you want every article to have your name, professional designation, address, and phone number on it. For anyone who finds one of your articles through a search engine or hypertext link rather than your home page, you also want to offer a quick and easy way of learning more about you and your practice. That is why every page should include a link back to your home page, as well as to other pages describing you and your practice or related information of potential use or interest.

Finally, you should register your site with the major search engines. Although search engines might find your site by accident, you should not rely on chance. Instead, ask to be indexed and included among the pages listed by the search engine. Most search engines have an easy way to make this request through their Web sites. A few Web sites will automatically register your site with most of the major search engines by filling out one simple on-line form. (See, for example, **http://www.submitit.com**.)

What's the Plan?

As explained in Chapter 1, marketing is usually more effective if efforts are concentrated on a specific target rather than scattered. Defining a practice area that leads to certain specific marketing efforts may therefore be more effective than general, unfocused marketing. Accordingly, you don't want to spend time and money on all of the marketing ideas in this chapter, only on those activities that suit you and your practice.

Planning your practice and the marketing for it need to go hand in hand. Ideally, you will settle into a type of practice that suits your personality and preferences (and your community's needs) but is also most effectively marketed in ways that best suit your personality and preferences.

The combination of the plan for your practice and the plan for marketing your practice is usually called a strategic plan or business plan. It can be as simple as a concept that a solo practitioner carries around in his or her head or as formal as a multipage memorandum developed by a committee within your firm and approved by the partners of the firm. For additional information on creating a strategic plan for a firm, department within a firm, or individual lawyer, see Robert W. Denney and Carol Scott James, *Action Steps to Marketing Success: How to Implement Your Marketing Program*, published by the ABA Law Practice Management Section.

Ethics Issues 3

Every experienced lawyer has an instinctive way of knowing when to turn a case down. For some, it's as subtle as a twitch in the vicinity of the forehead. For others, it's a complete loss of bladder control. For me, it's the knot that develops somewhere near my stomach and gradually spreads to my entire neuromuscular system, the only known antidote being the words, "you ought to seek other counsel."

—S. Sponte, Esq. (David J. Millstein),
The Collected Humor of an Uncollected Mind

NOTHING CAN BE SO DISTRACTING to a legal practice, or so potentially detrimental to a reputation in the community, as a malpractice action or complaint arising from a family conflict that does not involve your family but in which you are nevertheless ensnared. And nothing can generate a family conflict like an estate.

Chapter 2 discusses how to find clients. This chapter relates some of the reasons to turn down the clients you find or, if you accept them as clients, how to proceed with the care you need to keep the clients you want to keep and stay out of trouble. Unfortunately, many of the ABA *Model Rules of Professional Conduct,* which have been adopted in one form or another by more than two-thirds of the states, were written with litigators or business lawyers in mind and have an uncertain application to estate planners. (See "American College of Trust and Estate Counsel Commentaries on the Model Rules of Professional Conduct," 28 *Real Property, Probate, and Trust Law Journal* 865 (1994).) That, together with the inherent problems in providing clear ethics guidelines, means that often no clear answers to ethics problems exist. This chapter attempts to suggest some possible solutions to some common problems.

Conflicts of Interest

Conflicts of interest are exceedingly common in estate planning and estate administration. They are also commonly overlooked.

Conflicts of interest are common because estates lawyers frequently take on the role of the "family lawyer," trying to do what is in the family's best interests. That same desire to act as an advisor to the entire family also leads lawyers to ignore (or try to downplay) possible conflicts of interest within the family. Acting as a family advisor works as long as the family agrees on what is best, but if there are disagreements within the family, the lawyer will often be blamed for taking sides or failing to keep the disgruntled family members properly advised. The comments to Model Rule 2.2 sagely caution that, if a common representation fails, "the result can be additional cost, embarrassment, and recrimination."

When acting as a family advisor, and even when representing a husband and wife, the estates lawyer may be acting as an "intermediary" within the meaning of Model Rule 2.2. The comments to Model Rule 2.2 clearly state that an "intermediary" is not limited to arbitration or formal mediation but can include any situation in which the lawyer is helping to establish or adjust a relationship between clients, such as in starting a business or settling an estate. If Model Rule 2.2 applies, then the following applies:

- ◆ The lawyer must consult with each client about the possible risks and advantages of the common representation, including the effect on the attorney-client privilege, and obtain each client's consent. (Model Rule 2.2(a)(1).)

- The lawyer must reasonably believe that the common representation can be in each client's best interests and that each client will be able to make adequately informed decisions. (Model Rule 2.2(a)(2).)
- The lawyer must consult with each client concerning the decisions to be made, so that each client can make an adequately informed decision. (Model Rule 2.2(b).) This means that the lawyer cannot allow one client to withhold relevant facts from the other and may require disclosures to a client that are contrary to the usual expectation of attorney-client confidentiality toward another client.
- The lawyer must withdraw if any client requests or if conflicts make the continuing common representation inappropriate and, after withdrawal, the lawyer may not continue to represent any of the clients in the matter that was the subject of the common representation. (Model Rule 2.2(c).)

Because of Model Rule 2.2, as well as the potential conflicts in representing multiple members of the same family under Model Rules 1.7 and 1.9, many commentators recommend written disclosures and consents from each family member. Such formal written "solutions" aren't really what clients want or expect and aren't always necessary because the rules themselves do not require *written* consents. An oral consent may be appropriate in many cases. The sensibilities of most practitioners suggest a kind of "sliding scale" of disclosures and consents—that is, not making any express warnings or disclosures (not even oral) when the family's interests appear to be completely synchronous; making simple and low-key oral disclosures when there is a possibility of future differences or confusion over the lawyer's role; and delivering explicit oral warnings and possibly asking for written consents when there are clearly differing interests within the family, even though the family members are currently harmonious, because of the possibility that attitudes will change and compromises will fail.

The following are some common potential conflicts of interest, and some suggested approaches to the disclosures and consents that may be required under Model Rules 1.7, 1.9, and 2.2.

Husbands and Wives

One of the most difficult conflicts of interest is also the most common: the joint representation of a husband and wife. The sources of conflicts include possible differences in the dispositions of their estates and possible conflicts in the division and ownership of their assets during their lifetimes.

When either (or both) the husband and wife have children from other marriages, they may have different beneficiaries in mind for their estates as well as different estate planning goals. Because their interests are not the same, there are potential conflicts of interest. There may be conflicts even when there are no children because the spouses may have different ideas about benefits to parents, brothers, and sisters from their families of origin. When there are no children, many husbands and wives will try to agree on reciprocal wills that distribute the combined estates to one family or the other, or divide the estates between the two families, after the surviving spouse has died. Such reciprocal wills can lead to many different kinds of future misunderstandings and conflicts if it is not made absolutely clear to the clients and in the documents that the survivor is not legally bound by the agreement.

Even without differences over beneficiaries, there may be conflicts between a husband and wife about the management of their assets during their lifetimes or during the lifetime of the surviving spouse. Although transfers of assets between husband and wife, or to and from joint names, are frequently recommended in estate planning, those recommendations could adversely affect a spouse's interests in the event of a future divorce. They could also adversely affect the financial security of one spouse if the other became estranged, incompetent, irresponsible, or insolvent. In a community-property state, there may be questions about the identification of separate property and community property and the differing financial interests of the two spouses. Lastly, even happily married couples may find it difficult to talk about whether one of them might remarry after the death of the other and whether a marital deduction trust might be appropriate to protect their children from a second marriage or a future lover.

In a joint representation of a husband and wife, a lawyer should also be concerned about whether both spouses will be able to make "adequately informed decisions" (Model Rule 2.2(a)(2)) and whether the common representation can be "undertaken impartially" (Model Rule 2.2(a)(3)). Although more women nowadays are economically self-sufficient and financially knowledgeable, many marriages are still not equal partnerships and one spouse may control more of the family wealth, whether owing to inheritance, skill, hard work, or just plain luck. That spouse may follow the "golden rule" that "he who has the gold, makes the rules." Thus, any joint representation has in it the danger that you are not really representing both spouses—just the more vocal and assertive spouse—and that the other spouse is being pressured into decisions that he or she will later resent. If one of the spouses is a good friend or an important client, there is also the danger that you will pay more attention to the wishes and interests of the client with whom you have the more important relationship and will fail to consider the interests of both spouses impartially. In some cases, you may not be able to claim in good faith to be representing both parties.

Confidences in Joint Representations

Even if you have been able to tiptoe through the minefield of estate planning with a married couple, one of them may still be able to trip you at the end, or grab you and drag you back into the middle of the minefield.

Imagine that you have gotten through a somewhat tense estate planning meeting with a husband and wife who have different ideas about their estate plans but have a stubborn desire to reach an agreement on a common plan. You draft documents. The documents are signed. Then the husband phones to say that he wants to change his will to make provisions for his mistress. Or the wife phones to say that she's changed her mind and doesn't trust her husband controlling her estate, so she wants to name trustees to manage his inheritance for him. Now what?

If your representation is really a joint representation or intermediation within Model Rule 2.2, you may have an ethical obligation to inform the other spouse of the change in plans. In a joint representation, you are required to advise both parties regarding all decisions and supply them with all relevant information. On the other hand, if you are actually representing the husband and wife individually, you have an ethical obligation *not* to inform the other spouse. So you could be damned if you do, and damned if you don't. Now, don't you wish you knew whether the representation was joint or separate?

Another question is whether the representation has ended or is continuing. Do you still need to advise your clients of changes in circumstances, even after the documents have been signed?

Termination of a Joint Representation

Suppose that your clients end up reaching an impasse. They can neither agree nor agree to disagree, and you have decided that you can no longer represent both of them together. Under those circumstances, Model Rule 2.2(c) states that you cannot continue to represent either of them "in the matter that was the subject of the intermediation." Does that mean that you can't now complete any estate planning for either of them? That isn't always necessary because their estate planning could proceed separately, and yet Model Rule 2.2 requires it unless each of them agrees to allow you to continue to represent the other.

Disclosures and Consents

Most of the problems just described can be resolved (but not always avoided) if it is clearly established whether the representation of the husband and wife is a joint or common representation or separate and independent.

When the husband and wife have children together (and therefore the same beneficiaries), have a long and stable marriage, are both capable of managing their own finances and decisions, and come to you with similar ideas for the disposition of their estates, there would seem to be no conflict of interest between them. Little or no reason exists to make any disclosures about potential conflicts of interest or to request any express consents of the kind described in Model Rule 2.2. In fact, if the clients are not looking to the lawyer to advise them in establishing or adjusting their relationship, or in resolving a financial relationship, Rule 2.2 may not even apply.

Even when a husband and wife have different estate planning goals, whether because they have children from different marriages or similar reasons or because they have kept their finances separate in accordance with a marital agreement that limits rights in divorce or at death, there may be no problem because they have "agreed to disagree" and have different estate plans. In that case, it would be prudent to discuss the limits of the lawyer's role and the problems that could arise if there were disagreements, but it may not be necessary to get written waivers or consents.

The most difficult situation is when the spouses have differing estate planning goals and are looking to the lawyer to help them develop a common estate plan to accomplish those goals. In that case, it is necessary to discuss with them the problems that may arise in that kind of intermediation and to get their agreement to the form of the representation. A written agreement should also be considered.

When defining whether the representation of a husband and wife should be considered to be joint representation or intermediation within Model Rule 2.2 or should be considered to be two separate representations, it may be better (at least for the lawyer) to specify that the representations are separate. Then there is no obligation to share confidences with both spouses and fewer restrictions on continuing to represent both spouses even after a dispute or divorce. The form of estate planning fee agreement in Appendix B includes language that may be appropriate to an estate planning engagement by a husband and wife. (Many lawyers concerned about these issues believe that it may be advisable to get waivers and consents from married clients in every case, which is why the estate planning agreement in Appendix B includes this language.)

For additional considerations in the representations of husband and wives in estate planning, see "Report of the Special Study Committee on Professional Responsibility: Comments and Recommendations on the Lawyer's Duties in Representing Husband and Wife," 28 *Real Property, Probate, and Trust Law Journal* 765 (1994).

Business Planning

Consider the common problems in business (and farm) succession planning. When the business is a large part of the estate but only some of the heirs are active in managing the business, problems often occur in getting the business interests to the active heirs and comparable value to the inactive heirs. A possible solution is a buy-sell agreement, but if you prepare an agreement, who is your client? The present controlling owners? The younger generation? The business itself? One of them? Some of them? All of them?

Many estate planning lawyers represent all of the shareholders of a family-owned business. Let's say that you have done estate planning for each of the shareholders (perhaps parents and children, or maybe brothers or sisters who are equal owners) and some tax work for the corporation. You are sitting at a meeting of the shareholders or directors when an argument erupts and they all turn to you for advice. What do you say? Do you choose sides, or do you clear your throat, excuse yourself for a moment, leave the room, and not come back?

When you have represented several people (or entities) and you wear many different hats, your role can shift from meeting to meeting or conversation to conversation. You must remember whom you are advising and representing at the moment. You must also remind your clients of whom you are representing and what you consider your role to be at that moment. This can often be done subtly and tactfully, but it must sometimes be done more clearly and directly. It depends on the circumstances.

Suppose, for example, that the parents have decided that they want a buy-sell or redemption agreement with the corporation, of which their adult children are already voting shareholders. You have some meetings with the parents alone and they settle on terms that they think are fair. At this point, they ask you to meet with the children (for whom you have also done estate planning) and explain the agreement. When you meet with the children, you don't want to ask for a written disclaimer or waiver and you don't want to recommend that the children seek other counsel. You can nonetheless clearly and gently declare whom it is you represent by advising the children that you have been meeting with their parents and that their parents have asked you to meet with them to review the agreement. You can even go so far as to point out that you drafted the agreement and are actually representing the parents, but that you can explain the agreement and answer the children's questions even if you cannot give them truly impartial legal advice. If the children have any sense, you will get nods of under-standing and confirmation that they understand your role. If you do not get the confirmation that you need, you may have to push the disclosure process up a notch and talk about written disclaimers of conflicts.

Similarly, if you are in a meeting of shareholders and you have represented (or are representing) some or all of them individually, you can respond to a request for advice from one shareholder by reminding everyone that you are attending the meeting as counsel to the corporation and it would not be proper to represent any one shareholder or to advocate one particular position, although you can answer general questions about the consequences of what is being discussed. In other words, your role is to level the playing field by ensuring that each shareholder has the same information, but you are not supposed to advocate a particular position (although you may suggest a position that you believe is best for most of the shareholders). This is a classic form of intermediation within the meaning of Model Rule 2.2. If any of your clients are not satisfied with that role, you should withdraw from the meeting, and from any representation of the corporation, until the conflict is resolved. (See Model Rules 1.13, 1.9, and 2.2.)

Other Generational Conflicts

Other conflicts can arise when the parents decide on estate plans that do not treat the children equally, that create trusts for children because of perceived problems in maturity, emotional stabil-ity, substance abuse, or other shortcomings, or that decide to "skip a generation" when the generation does not want to be skipped. These situations can create problems if the same lawyer is trying to do estate planning for both generations. In addition, anger and resentment can result if the same lawyer who helped draft the unwanted estate plan is in charge of administering it when the parents are no longer there to explain their decisions.

Conflicts of interest clearly exist when there are financial trans-actions between the generations, as illustrated in the earlier discus-sion of business planning. Yet is there really a conflict of interest in meeting separately with different generations and preparing sepa-rate wills or trusts for them? The comments to Model Rule 1.7

include the suggestion that a conflict *may* arise when preparing wills for several family members "under some circumstances," but they do not explain *what* circumstances. Commentators also have concluded that conflicts of interest can exist in estate planning for different generations. (See, for example, Jeffrey N. Pennell, "Professional Responsibility: Reforms Are Needed to Accommodate Estate Planning and Family Counselling," *University of Miami Institute on Estate Planning* (Vol. 25, 1991).) However, while the interests of different generations may be *different*, it is not clear that they are *adverse* within the meaning of Model Rule 1.7.

Most conflicts of interest involve conflicting financial or property interests. The general (and historical) rule, however, is that a person cannot have a property interest in the estate of a living person or in a gift that has not yet been made. This general rule has been eroded by recent exceptions that allow beneficiaries of a client to sue an estate planner for malpractice after the client has died and disappointed beneficiaries to sue successful beneficiaries for "tortious interference with the right of inheritance." The author is not yet aware of any published opinion that an interest in the estate of a living person is enough to create an adverse interest under the rules relating to conflicts of interest.

Another problem with the concept of estate planning conflicts of interest between generations is that most of the examples seem to be problems of confidentiality, not conflicts of interest. For example, a lawyer prepares a will or trust for a parent contrary to what one of the children wants and then keeps it a secret from the child while doing estate planning for the child. The child may be angry when the parent dies and the estate plan becomes public knowledge, but the lawyer could not have disclosed anything to the child without violating the duty of confidentiality to the parent. Similarly, the lawyer may represent a child and discover things about the child's private life that would cause the parent to change his or her will and yet not be able to tell the parent without violating the child's confidences. While these situations put the lawyer into the difficult situation of having knowledge about one client that cannot be shared with another client, the situation is not much different from a lawyer who acquires "insider information" about a client company that cannot be shared with other clients who are actual or potential investors.

Although intrafamily interests are not necessarily adverse within the meaning of Model Rule 1.7(a), it is still possible that relationships with different family members may "materially limit" the representation of another family member within the meaning of Model Rule 1.7(b). For example, it is a common part of estate planning for a person with living parents to ask about the parents' estate plans so that the child's planning can anticipate any inheritances or exercise any powers given to the child. If the lawyer already represents the parents and knows that the parents do not wish for the child to know about the decisions they have made, the lawyer may be limited in his or her ability to encourage the child to seek this information. Even if this is not an actual conflict of interest, it at least creates an appearance of impropriety.

It is quite common for estates lawyers to represent several generations without encountering any conflicts of interest, there being little or no secrecy and nothing in particular to keep secret. A lawyer should be able to represent and advise different generations of the same family in their individual estate planning as long as the lawyer is able to keep the confidences of each generation separate and can exercise independent professional judgment within the meaning of Model Rule 2.1. However, a lawyer should avoid representing different members of the same family when there are family secrets or emotional conflicts between them and different estate planning objectives. It is simply too easy for that kind of situation to erupt into an estate dispute with the lawyer in the middle.

Representation of Fiduciary-Beneficiaries

Problems arise in estate administrations when you represent an executor (or trustee) who is also a beneficiary. One possible dilemma arises when you represent the surviving spouse as executor and realize that the surviving spouse might be better off (or at least might prefer) to elect against the will rather than take the limited interests it provides. In some jurisdictions, the lawyer for the estate has fiduciary obligations to the beneficiaries, so if you advise the surviving spouse to elect against the will, the other estate beneficiaries may complain that you have favored the surviving spouse and failed to treat all of the beneficiaries impartially.

You have also counseled a client to act against the will that, as the lawyer for the executor, you are supposed to execute and defend. If you should decide not to advise the surviving spouse to elect against the will, you will have failed in your duty to your client as a beneficiary. The author believes that most lawyers in this situation would advise the surviving spouse to elect because the obligation to the surviving spouse is clearer than any obligation to the other beneficiaries.

Other questions can arise when the executor has the power to make tax elections that may affect the distribution of the estate in which the executor has an interest. Must the consequences of each decision be explained to all of the beneficiaries? Must you explain only those decisions that benefit the fiduciary-beneficiary? Or is there no duty to explain anything at all to the other beneficiaries? Most lawyers who have considered these issues will err on the side of disclosure and send each beneficiary a full explanation of each decision made and the consequences of the decision.

Ultimately, conflicts among beneficiaries can arise that make it impossible to continue to claim to be advising the fiduciary impartially while also serving as an advocate for the same client as beneficiary. In such cases, it may be necessary to choose whether you wish to represent the client as fiduciary or the client as beneficiary. This choice is common in estate litigation in Pennsylvania, where courts often require a fiduciary-beneficiary to retain two different lawyers, one to represent him or her in the fiduciary capacity and one to represent his or her interests as a beneficiary. At a minimum, this separation of counsel ensures that the estate is not paying legal fees to represent the fiduciary's personal interests as a beneficiary.

Questions about the estate can extend to estate planning decisions made during the decedent's lifetime. If you were the estate planner and questions arise about the tax planning or the decedent's true intentions, you may have to defend your own documents or recommendations against complaints by some or all of the beneficiaries. If those documents or recommendations benefited your current client (the fiduciary-beneficiary), there may be conflicts between or among your interests (e.g., possible malpractice in the estate planning), the interests of your present client, and the interests of the other estate beneficiaries. Such problems may require total withdrawal from the representation of the client, both as a fiduciary and as a beneficiary.

Relations with Client-Beneficiaries

Another common situation is the representation of a fiduciary of an estate or trust that benefits present or former clients. For example, you may have helped the adult children of a client with their own estate planning and may then become the lawyer for the executor or trustee for their deceased parent. In that situation, it is easy for the children (your present or former clients) to believe that you will be representing their interests in the estate's administration. It may be perfectly appropriate for you to act as an intermediary consistent with Model Rule 2.2 and provide the legal advice that the family (both fiduciaries and beneficiaries) need to settle the estate or trust to their mutual satisfaction. This is, however, a situation in which clarity is essential.

If you are willing to act as an intermediary within the meaning of Model Rule 2.2, you should confirm to all of your clients, preferably in writing, that you will be acting in that role. You should also advise them of the consequences of that role (e.g., that you will not be able to represent any of them with respect to the estate or trust, including the fiduciary, if a dispute should arise among them that cannot be resolved without separate counsel). If you are *not* acting as an intermediary but representing only the fiduciary, you must advise your beneficiary-clients of that fact and seek their consent, preferably in writing, to your representation of the fiduciary even though that representation may be adverse to their interests. (See Model Rules 1.7 and 1.9.)

Relations with Unrepresented Beneficiaries

Even when representing only a fiduciary without any beneficial interest in the estate, and when there are no current or prior relationships with any beneficiaries, there are still troubling questions about obligations to the beneficiaries. Does the lawyer for the fiduciary have any obligation to the beneficiaries to inform them of tax elections or other rights available to them? For example, does the lawyer for an estate have an obligation to the beneficiaries to advise them about the possibility of disclaimers of their interests which may be beneficial if, for example, the beneficiaries would like to make gifts to their children and the result of disclaimers would be the same as tax-free gifts to the children?

This problem is specifically recognized in the following comment from Model Rule 1.7:

> In estate administration the identity of the client may be unclear under the law of a particular jurisdiction. Under one view, the client is the fiduciary; under another view the client is the estate or trust, including its beneficiaries. The lawyer should make clear the relationship to the parties involved.

To "make clear the relationship" and avoid possible misunderstandings, you should write to the beneficiaries, preferably in one of your first letters or notices to them, and advise them that you represent the fiduciary (if that is consistent with local law), and that you will provide appropriate information about the estate as requested. You should state that the beneficiary should consult with a lawyer or accountant about the tax or legal consequences of distributions by the fiduciary, or if there are any questions about their rights in the estate.

Elderly or Infirm Clients

One situation specifically addressed by the *Model Rules of Professional Conduct* is the problem of dealing with clients under a disability. Model Rule 1.14(a) states that a lawyer should "as far as reasonably possible" maintain a normal lawyer-client relationship with a client whose decision-making ability is impaired. Rule 1.14(b) provides that a lawyer may seek the appointment of a guardian or take other action to protect a client only when the lawyer reasonably believes that the client cannot reasonably act in the client's own interests.

Unfortunately, the more difficult (and dangerous) situations are those in which the client is aged or infirm and may be subject to undue influence by other family members in the execution of wills, trusts, gifts, and other estate planning matters. Nothing gets an experienced lawyer's antennae quivering quite like being asked to prepare documents for someone other than the person making the request or meeting with an elderly client who wants to favor the child who is present at the meeting and disinherit a child who is absent. These situations are legal powder kegs.

Every lawyer must insist on meeting with the client for whom a will or trust is prepared and also on meeting with a client alone and outside of the presence of any beneficiary on whom the client wants to bestow a special benefit. Only in a private meeting can the lawyer find out what the client wants to do and why and make an independent assessment of whether the client might be acting under undue influence.

A well-known client who asks you to prepare reciprocal wills for herself and her husband should not be a problem, nor should a child asking about a will for an elderly parent if you have met with the parent before and the family dynamics are known to you. However, preparing important or unusual documents for people you don't know well, or don't know at all, is never a good idea.

Confidentiality

In both estate planning and estate administration, lawyers are exposed to some of the most intimate details of their clients' lives. Marital indiscretions, children born out of wedlock, substance abuse, emotional and physical disabilities, family fights, and other personal information is frequently discussed with a lawyer during estate planning or administration. In addition, most people consider their finances and estate plans to be among their most personal and private affairs.

To inspire the confidence of your clients and to avoid a possible breach of legal ethics, paranoia is the best policy. The following guidelines may be helpful:

- ◆ Never tell your spouse anything about mutual friends or family members. You obviously shouldn't tell your spouse the names of your clients without their consent but, if you're representing friends or family members, they may talk to your spouse about you and your work, so your spouse may know without your saying anything. Even so, you should still keep your professional contacts with friends or relations as secret as possible because slips and misunderstandings are all too easy. Suppose that you and your husband are both friends with Bill, who calls to ask for your advice about a situation that is obviously confidential. You meet for lunch, during which you also exchange some family chitchat, such as that Bill's child has been admitted to college. That night, you mention to your husband that you saw Bill for lunch, and you relate some of the family chitchat. Your husband later sees Bill and congratulates him on the college news. Now, Bill knows that the college news came up at the same lunch as the confidential matter about which he is worried. It would be natural for him to wonder what else you might have told your husband and to begin worrying that his personal problems are a source of family gossip. That sort of worrying drives away both clients and friends, and it is completely avoidable. Tell your husband or wife absolutely nothing! That will eliminate the possibility of any misunderstanding.

◆ Never say anything about the client's affairs to anyone but the client without the client's express permission. This may seem obvious, but it is easy to be led astray by accountants, life insurance agents, and other advisors who may phone to ask you something about the client's assets or arrangements.

◆ Never tell any of the client's employees why you are calling. When you call a business executive or a doctor or other professional about personal estate matters, there is simply no reason to tell a secretary, receptionist, or any other employee why you are calling. It is none of their business, and your client may consider it to be confidential. Whether your clients have a will or trust, or whether they even have an estate large enough to be worth planning, is simply not something you should disclose without your client's permission. You should never leave any message or provide any explanation of your call beyond the fact that you are a lawyer and you believe that the person you are calling will want to speak with you. (I am occasionally amused by doctors' receptionists who want to know why I'm calling and aren't willing to accept my explanation that it is "personal." It often takes the receptionist a while to understand that I'm not trying to avoid talking about my own medical problem and that it is personal to the doctor, not to me.)

◆ Never mail or fax anything to a client's business without confirming it with the client in advance. Many clients do not want personal information going through the mail room, being opened by secretaries, or sitting on a fax machine in their office. Many others don't care. Don't guess. Ask.

◆ Never tell your clients anecdotes about other cases. It is sometimes tempting to illustrate an explanation to a client with a story about another case or situation you handled, but it is usually a mistake. Even though you have not named any names and everything is a matter of public record in pleadings or court accounts, the client may still view your story as a kind of gossiping and worry that his or her story may be subject to the same fate.

Your employees must keep client confidences as well. These same rules apply to your employees, and it is your job to instruct and supervise them. (See Model Rule 5.3.)

Lawyers' Trust Accounts

Do *not* put trust funds into a law firm's trust account. So-called trust accounts have nothing to do with trusts. Instead, they are intended to hold client funds that come into the possession of a law firm as a result of settlement payments, real estate and business closings, advances by clients of unearned fees, escrows, and other matters having nothing to do with estates and trusts.

Under the laws of most states, any funds held by a lawyer as an executor or trustee must be segregated in separate accounts and must *not* be commingled with the lawyer's own funds or with the funds of any other estate or trust. That fiduciary duty dictates that estate and trust funds not be held in firm trust accounts. Only banks and trust companies may establish common trust funds in which the funds of several estates or trusts may be invested. Those funds are more like money market or mutual funds than shared bank accounts.

A typical estates and trusts lawyer will probably require the use of a lawyer trust account only in the following cases:

- ◆ Advances for costs or fees received from the client but not yet earned. (See Chapter 4.)
- ◆ Sales by estates or trusts of real estate business interests during which checks must be collected, deposited, cleared, and then disbursed at settlement.
- ◆ Funds received by an estate but not part of an estate, such as funds or other property in the possession of the decedent but not owned by the decedent.
- ◆ Disputed fees pending resolution of the dispute.

For additional information about the proper use and management of lawyer trust accounts, see *The ABA Guide to Lawyer Trust Accounts* by Jay G Foonberg, published by the ABA Law Practice Management Section.

Necessary Vigilance

Estates lawyers are probably entrusted with the most personal of confidences and are probably more entangled in potential conflicts of interest than lawyers in any other field. Yet there are probably fewer complaints against estates lawyers and less scrutiny than in other fields. This must be considered to be a tribute to the tact, discretion, and good sense of most estates lawyers. However, practitioners must remain vigilant in watching for potential conflicts of interest among their clients, and they must periodically remind their multiple clients just who it is that they are really representing and whether (and when) they are serving as counselors, as advocates, or as intermediaries.

Fees and Fee Agreements 4

Work expands so as to fill the time available for its completion.

—Cyril Northcote Parkinson,
Parkinson's Law, or the
Pursuit of Progress

Time is what you measure when nothing else is happening.

—Richard P. Feynman,
Lectures in Physics

MOST LAWYERS DO NOT LIKE TO BILL. It may be because of the time required to review time records and preliminary bills, or it may be because of a fear that the client won't like the bill, but the legal aversion to billing is epidemic. In fact, the most common complaint that I hear from friends and acquaintances about bills from lawyers is not about the bill's *size* but rather its *lateness*. Many clients are confused by bills received from lawyers in December for work done in January (perhaps even the January of the year before).

We could speculate about the psychological factors that cause lawyers to procrastinate about billing, but it clearly represents a great misunderstanding by lawyers of their proper role. Many lawyers think that their job is to win cases, make deals, or give advice. That is too narrow and is tremendously short-sighted. A lawyer's real job is to reduce the number and severity of the client's problems, and legal costs are a problem that must be taken into account for all clients. It is foolish to say that a lawyer has won a suit but the client isn't happy with the result, particularly if the client isn't happy with the result because the lawyer's bill is higher than the client expected or can afford. The lawyer has not solved the client's problem, but instead has exchanged one problem (the lawsuit) for another problem (the bill).

Billing is not incidental to the practice of law or a necessary evil. It is an integral part of any legal representation and the only way to measure our success as lawyers. If we properly advise our clients, pay attention to their needs and goals, estimate costs accurately, and manage our time effectively, our clients will be satisfied and will show their satisfaction by paying our bills.

That is why I look forward to billing my clients. It is when I learn whether I have been successful. Billing is my report card from my clients.

Fee Agreements

Rule 1.5(b) of the ABA *Model Rules of Professional Conduct* states, "When the lawyer has not regularly represented the client, the basis or rate of the fee shall be communicated to the client, preferably in writing, before or within a reasonable time after commencing the representation." Some states have modified the rule to provide that fee agreements *must* be in writing.

Regardless of ethics rules (or even possible legal problems in collecting fees without an agreement), providing clear fee agreements is simply good business. A client who agrees in advance to a particular fee is less likely to be surprised when the fee is actually billed—and is more likely to pay—than a client who has little idea of what fee will be charged.

Further, fee discussions with clients help to build mutual trust and respect. Failure to discuss fees with clients could be viewed by the client as patronizing or insulting, suggesting that the client is too ignorant, naive, or foolish to make a sound judgment about what is or is not an appropriate fee, or that the client is basically helpless to affect the amount of the fee and must accept whatever arrangement the lawyer imposes. Fee discussions can be empowering for the client, affirming that the client has power to make decisions and that the lawyer will respect the client's decisions and judgments. Talking to your client about your fees is not a necessary evil but an opportunity to treat your client with respect and to impress your client with your good business sense.

Clear and concise fee agreements are particularly appropriate to estate planning and estate administration representations, which frequently consist of specific tasks and are usually of relatively short duration.

The Basis or Rate of the Fee

Currently a hot topic in law practice management is the issue of alternative billing strategies. If we don't bill by the hour, how do we bill? What is value billing (and what is "value")?

The problems with hourly billing and the advantages of alternative billing are set forth in *Beyond the Billable Hour: An Anthology of Alternative Billing Methods* and *Win-Win Billing Strategies,* both edited by Richard C. Reed and published by the ABA Law Practice Management Section. Briefly, the problems with hourly billing include the following:

- ◆ Hourly billing promotes inefficiency, both on individual client matters and within the firm. Hourly billing can result in a nightmarish application of Parkinson's Law. Work expands to fill the time allowed, but there is no clear limit on the time allowed and the client is billed for the time that was spent rather than the result or the benefit to the client.
- ◆ Most clients don't like hourly billing because of the perceived inefficiency (i.e., the client knows that he or she is being billed for time the lawyer wastes) as well as the uncertainty (i.e., the client may feel that he or she is writing a "blank check" to the lawyer).

- ◆ A strictly hourly fee may not be ethical because it is only *one* of the eight factors to be considered in determining the reasonableness of a fee under Rule 1.5(a) of the *Model Rules of Professional Conduct.*
- ◆ In hourly billing, the financial interests of the lawyer and the client actually conflict. The lawyer has an interest in extending the conflict or representation and spending more time than is necessary, while the client would prefer a speedy result and economy in time spent. Hourly billing therefore increases the likelihood of fee disputes between lawyer and client and undermines the lawyer-client relationship.

The following are among the alternatives to traditional hourly billing:

- ◆ Fixed-fee billing, in which specific dollar values are assigned to particular transactions or representations.
- ◆ Contingent fee or other results-oriented billing, in which the lawyer's fee is measured by the financial benefit obtained by the client (or the financial loss avoided by the client).
- ◆ Budgeted billing, in which the lawyer prepares specific budgets for the time to be spent on the matter and must be able to explain (and justify) variations from the budget.
- ◆ Blended-rate billing, in which the client agrees to pay specific hourly rates for specific tasks, regardless of who performs the tasks, which gives the firm an incentive to perform the work using the personnel with the lowest billing rates.

One conclusion that seems to follow from most case studies and discussions of alternative billing methods is that no one billing strategy will necessarily apply to all types of representations or practice areas. There is no one-size-fits-all method of value billing, but it seems that some common types of representations should be dealt with through a form or formula that will yield the "right" fee in most cases.

In many areas of estate planning and estate and trust administration, a combination of billing methods can work well together to provide a fee arrangement that is better than simple hourly billing for both the lawyer and the client.

Alternative Billing in Estate Planning

Estate planning typically proceeds in two stages, although there is often overlap between the stages. The first stage is deciding what to do, which requires consideration of the client's circumstances and may also require tax calculations and tax or other legal research and analysis. Once the lawyer and client have agreed on what to do, the second stage is to do whatever is needed to carry out the decisions, which may require drafting documents, transferring assets, and other steps to implement the estate plan.

Fees for the Initial Meeting

An important first question is whether to charge a fee for the initial client meeting. A "free" initial meeting may be very attractive to clients who worry about making fee commitments without knowing anything about estate planning or what legal services are really needed (or whether any services are really needed).

I have put the word "free" in quotation marks because the first meeting is not really free. The cost of the meeting will be included in the fees for the services upon which the client agrees. There is, however, no *obligation* to pay any fee until the client's situation has been discussed and the lawyer's services and fees for those services have been agreed to, and that is what is important to the client. Offering free initial consultations may therefore be profitable enough in attracting new business to compensate for the cost of providing initial consultations to potential clients who never come back.

Fees for Analysis

In most cases, a lawyer will spend some time preparing or presenting recommendations for the client or preparing numeric projections illustrating the distribution of the client's estate and possible tax liabilities.

Fixed fees for the analysis and decision-making stage may be difficult to determine without knowing something about the client's estate planning goals and circumstances. In addition, time spent in client meetings to obtain information and to explain and discuss recommendations can be a significant part of the time needed for this stage of the planning process. The exact amount of time needed by a particular client may be affected by the client's personality and therefore difficult to determine in advance. Nevertheless, many estates lawyers try to avoid hourly billing and fix fees for estate planning recommendations in advance, through one or more of the following ways:

- ◆ **Fixed fee for a standard review:** One approach is to develop a fairly standard checklist of recommendations to be reviewed for each client and to charge a fixed fee for that standard estate planning review. Areas for such a review could include proper use of the unified credit and marital deductions upon the death of the first spouse of a married couple, lifetime giving using the annual exclusion and unified credit, unmet liquidity needs for death taxes, exclusion of life insurance from the taxable estate, and generation-skipping planning. This kind of fixed fee usually includes a set amount of time for client meetings, with additional charges at hourly rates if the client requires additional meetings. (Extraordinary needs and recommendations, such as business succession planning, use of a charitable split-interest trust, GRATs, and other planning issues could still be handled on an hourly basis if approved by the client.)

- ◆ **Estimated fee after an initial (no-obligation) meeting:** Another approach is to attempt to set the fees for the estate planning review only after the initial client meeting, for which there is no fee and no obligation unless the client agrees to additional services. After that initial meeting, the client's assets and personal objectives will be better known, so it should be possible to determine which estate planning issues and techniques to present to the client. The problem with this approach is that it may require at least three client meetings (one to determine the fees and goals for the planning process, one to review the plan, and another to execute documents), while many clients may not require that much lawyer time.

- ◆ **Implementation fees only:** A third approach is to charge nothing for the initial client meeting and the recommendations proposed and reviewed during that meeting and to base all fees on the documents and other steps needed to implement the recommendations approved by the client. The disadvantage of this approach is that clients may drop out of the planning process before making any decisions, so the lawyer will have spent time without receiving any fee. The advantage of this approach to the lawyer is that it may be possible to complete the estate planning process with only two meetings, an initial meeting to collect information, establish estate planning goals, settle on a recommended estate plan, and set a fee for the services, and a second to review and execute documents. The advantage to the client is that the client pays only for the estate plan the client actually chooses, so the client pays only for actual results. The form of fee agreement included in Appendix B was developed to be used with clients who are able to make estate planning decisions during the initial meeting so that the lawyer can set fees for the documents or other services to be rendered, complete the fee agreement by hand, and ask the clients to approve the fees before the meeting ends.

It is not necessary to use the same approach with all clients. The best procedure may be to meet with the client and determine whether an estate plan can be settled on during the meeting, with one additional meeting to review and execute documents (a two-meeting process), or whether it is necessary to prepare written recommendations (for a fee) and possibly meet again to review and discuss the recommendations before preparing documents, still needing a third meeting to execute the documents (a three-meeting process).

Fees for Documents and Implementation

Once the lawyer has made recommendations to the client and the client has made all the personal and tax decisions that go into an estate plan, the most time-consuming tasks are the drafting of the wills, trusts, powers of attorney, deeds, buy-sell agreements, and other contracts and documents to carry out the estate plan. Because the use and content of those documents should be established during the analysis stage, it should be possible to determine a fixed fee for preparing those documents. In determining the fee, you should consider the following factors:

- **Document complexity:** A larger, more complex document takes longer to review and proof even if the first draft is prepared with computerized drafting software. A document's complexity is also a sign of the technical sophistication needed to prepare the document and increased risk of technical errors or omissions that could result in professional liability. So, for example, wills with marital deduction provisions, trusts for children, or generation-skipping trusts should cost more than simpler wills.

◆ **Required customization:** Regardless of how sophisticated a computerized drafting system may be, a certain amount of customization must be made for each client. If the client's circumstances are out of the ordinary, such as stepchildren or other unusual family circumstances or special dispositions for business interests or other specific assets, special provisions may need to be drafted for the client. That kind of special drafting will take time for which there should be compensation.

◆ **Time needed for services after execution:** If in addition to the time needed to revise, execute, and complete the documents, the fixed fees for particular documents also include tasks that may be required to carry out the purpose of the documents after they are signed, the fee for the documents should include any additional time ordinarily needed for those tasks. For example, if the preparation of an irrevocable life insurance trust includes the application for an employer identification number for the trust, transfer of the life insurance policies, and instructions to the trustees regarding future payment of premiums, then the fee for the preparation of the trust should include those services.

The lawyer should be able to prepare guidelines for certain common forms of documents, based on the documents' complexity and the time usually needed to complete them, and then adjust the guideline fee for the time required to customize the documents for particular clients.

Fees for Second (or Third) Meetings

Regardless of how you decide to charge for preparing an estate plan and the documents required for the plan, you must remember that some clients need more explanations, conversations, or hand-holding than other clients. While it may be appropriate to include a certain average amount of meeting time in fixed fees, you should also be explicit about how much time is included in your fee schedule for meetings and telephone conversations and whether the client will be billed for excess time required by the client.

This is one area in which billing by the hour should be appropriate and agreeable to the client, because the client is really the one who determines the length and frequency of your conversations.

Alternative Billing Strategies in Estate Administrations

Traditionally, estate administration fees have been based on the value of the estate, and some states (e.g., New York and California) still have statutory schedules for lawyers' fees based on a percentage of the estate (usually a progressive scale, with the percentage of the estate becoming smaller as the estate gets larger). More recently, lawyers have been billing for estate administrations by the hour. Both methods have advantages and disadvantages.

Basing a fee on the size of estate can result in a reasonable fee, depending on the percentage applied and the composition of the estate, but it has been increasingly criticized by both clients and courts as arbitrary and not sufficiently related to the lawyer's time and efforts. Hourly billing is more closely related to the lawyer's time but, as with all other hourly billing, it leads to suspicions that the time has been padded or that the lawyer was not as efficient as he or she might have been had the meter not been running. Clients are also reluctant to engage a lawyer at an hourly rate with no clear idea of how much time will be spent or whether the final fee will be reasonable in relation to the size and nature of the estate.

Looking at the problem from a different perspective, a reasonable fee for most standard estate administrations might be determined from the number of transactions in the estate rather than the value of the estate. For example, it takes the same effort to value, administer, and distribute one thousand shares of stock in a corporation as it takes to administer ten shares of stock in the same corporation, because it takes about the same time and effort regardless of whether those shares are worth $10,000 or $10 million. It should therefore be possible to prepare an estate administration fee agreement in which the fees are based on the type of tasks necessary for the administration of the estate and, when appropriate, the number of assets or transactions involved in the administration.

In calculating fees for some tasks, it may be necessary to identify a "base fee" for the task as well as an incremental fee for transactions that add to the complexity of the task. For example, a death tax return requires a certain amount of time to prepare even if the return reports only one asset. For that reason, it may be appropriate to charge a fee for preparing the simplest possible return, with incremental fees for each asset or deduction that adds to the complexity of the return and the time needed to prepare it.

It is also a good idea to identify those tasks that might make other tasks easier and to provide discounts for the common elements of different tasks. For example, entry of an asset in the inventory of an estate requires information about the asset, including a description and the value upon the date of death. Entry of the same asset on the death tax return requires basically the same information. In fact, if the lawyer's office has computer programs to prepare fiduciary accounts and death tax returns and those programs can share asset information, entering the asset into one program may automatically enter the asset into the other program. In that case, the fee paid for entering assets into the fiduciary accounting system may cover most of the time and cost of entering the same asset into the death tax return. Therefore, it may be appropriate for the fee schedule for death tax returns to distinguish between probate assets (which are presumably already known and in the system) and nonprobate assets (such as life insurance, retirement benefits, and jointly owned property) for which descriptions and values still need to be determined independently of the fiduciary accounting system.

Another essential, though sometimes overlooked, goal of fixed-fee arrangements of this kind is to define precisely what *is* included in the regular or fixed fee and what is *not.* Unusual questions or problems may yet have to be billed on an hourly basis, and that needs to be spelled out in the fee agreement.

A possible form of fee agreement based on these considerations (but with no dollar amounts for the tasks or transactions) is given in Appendix C. The author has administered several estates using this type of fee arrangement, and the results have been good. Clients have been pleased to know that most of the fees are objectively determinable and predictable. Time records show a direct and predictable relationship between time spent and the actual fee charged. Although several of the dollar amounts originally included in the agreement needed to be revised upward (and one or two numbers needed to be revised downward), the basic approach is sound.

Alternative Billing Strategies in Litigation

In some types of estate litigation (or perhaps even tax litigation), the client may be unwilling to pay legal fees in the absence of a successful result. For example, a claimant to an estate may not be willing to pay large fees for the litigation necessary to prove the claim but may be willing to pay a larger than normal fee out of the fruits of a successful claim. Under such circumstances, estates lawyers may wish to consider the kinds of contingent fee agreements common to personal injury litigators.

One aspect of a contingent fee in estate litigation that would be different from fees in suits for personal injuries or other damages is that, in an estate contest, the amount to be recovered is usually either known or can be predicted in advance and is not a subject of dispute. In a will contest, the size of the estate is usually known, so what the client will receive if the will contest is successful can be predicted with some certainty. In personal injury litigation, by contrast, both the liability for the injury and the amount of compensation for the injury may be hotly disputed. So, a contingent fee in an estate matter is really a form of contingent fixed fee, not a variable fee, and the fee can end up being a kind of double-or-nothing gamble for the lawyer and the client

Other Terms and Conditions

In addition to the amount of the fee to be earned, fee agreements should cover several other issues.

Costs Advanced

The most consistently profitable activity for many firms is making photocopies. It may not be exciting, but it is a fee that is easy to bill and to collect. Nevertheless, many lawyers do not like to bill clients for those kinds of costs. After all, sending a bill that includes both $3,000 in fees and $23.47 for copying and postage might appear to be somewhat cheap or petty.

Whatever you decide to do, make sure that your fee agreement accurately reflects your policies. If your firm regularly marks up copying costs, on-line legal research fees, and other out-of-pocket costs, be sure that the markup is disclosed to the client in advance in the fee agreement. Otherwise, you have an agreement that refers to billings for "costs" and bills that list "costs" that are actually more than the costs paid by the firm, which is at least misleading and contrary to the fee agreement (if not unethical or downright fraudulent).

Payments in Advance

When fees are fixed in advance, it is much easier to ask for payment in advance, and payment in advance is obviously better for the lawyer. However, it raises technical problems.

In most jurisdictions, a fee paid by the client in advance is still considered to be the property of the client even though paid to the lawyer, and so it must be segregated and accounted for separately until the fee has been earned (and billed). (See Jay G Foonberg's *The ABA Guide to Lawyer Trust Accounts,* published by the ABA Law Practice Management Section.) This raises a number of bookkeeping complications for what may be, in many cases, relatively small amounts. To avoid these bookkeeping problems, some lawyers have described the relatively small payments in advance as "nonrefundable," or have attributed the payments to services already rendered, so that there is no "property of the client" to refund and nothing to segregate. For example, an estate planning lawyer might have an initial meeting with the client, make some recommendations, and quote a fee of $2,000 for the preparation of new wills or other documents, also requesting that half of the fee ($1,000) be paid as a nonrefundable advance, justifying the fee by the time already spent and recommendations already made during the initial meeting.

Another common area for advance billings is estate administrations. Most of the tasks in estate administrations have known deadlines, and many of the fees for those tasks can be set in advance, as described previously. For example, the federal estate tax return is due nine months from the date of death. The fee for preparing the return might be determined (or at least fairly accurately estimated) in advance, so that the fee for preparing the return could be billed in advance. In fact, some lawyers plan for quarterly billing of estate administration fees that cover the tasks expected to be performed over the following quarter. However, those advance billings may also be considered the property of the client under the ethics rules regarding trust accounts until the return is completed and the fee is earned.

Interest on Unpaid Fees and Costs

To encourage the client to pay the bill promptly, interest should be charged on bills remaining unpaid for thirty days or more. Federal and state law generally prohibit the assessment of interest unless agreed to in advance. It is therefore advisable to include provisions for interest on unpaid bills in your fee agreements.

Attorney's Liens

Some states allow what is called an attorney's lien or charging lien against property of the client in the hands of the lawyer. They allow the lawyer to retain the property if the lawyer's services were instrumental in acquiring the property, the client has not paid for the services, and the client will not be prejudiced by the property's retention. If your jurisdiction allows for such an attorney's lien and such a lien might be helpful in collecting unpaid fees, you might want to consider references to the possibility of the lien (and the lien's enforcement) in your fee agreements.

How to Write a Bill

Obviously, a bill should communicate to the client the fee that has been earned, any reimbursable costs incurred, and the total owed by the client.

Although it may not be legally or ethically required, good business practice—and good client relations—suggest that the bill also provide sufficient information to allow the client to verify that the fee imposed is consistent with the fee agreement. If the fee is supposed to be based on an hourly rate, the bill should show the time spent. If the fee agreement specified different hourly rates for different persons or different tasks, the bill should show who spent the time and what tasks were performed, so that the hourly rates can be verified. For a fee based on flat fees for particular documents prepared or tasks completed, the bill should identify which documents or tasks have been completed and the fees charged for those documents or tasks. The bill for a fee based on number of transactions recorded, the value of assets administered, or any basis other than time spent should disclose the number of transactions or the value of the assets, so that the client can compare the bill to the fee agreement and verify the fee.

A bill can also serve as a status report to a client, showing the time spent and the progress made during the preceding month. It is also a report in a form that the client may find particularly interesting because it allows the client to compare the progress during the past month with the cost of that progress.

A comprehensive book on writing bills is J. Harris Morgan's *How to Draft Bills Clients Rush to Pay,* from the ABA Law Practice Management Section. One of the book's important points is that bills should emphasize the *value* of what you've accomplished, not merely the time you've spent. Bills are an opportunity to communicate to your clients the value of your services. Use that opportunity to emphasize the substance of what was done rather than the way in which the time was spent.

For example, you could prepare a bill that reports a half hour in "telephone conversation with an IRS auditor to discuss valuation of business interests in taxable estate." Alternatively, you could report a half hour with the IRS "presenting evidence of lower valuation for business interests" or, even better, "resulting in lower valuation of business interests, for tax saving of approximately $80,000." If you were a client, which description would lead you to believe that you had received value for the fee you were paying?

The following pointers may be helpful:

◆ Use active verbs and strong, precise nouns, not vague, passive words. This general rule of good writing applies to bills as well as journalism and creative writing. For example, do not merely report a "conference with opposing counsel regarding legal issues." Instead, describe a "presentation to opposing counsel of the statutes and cases supporting our position," so that the client has a clearer notion of the actions you took and the purpose and value of your actions. "Presentation" suggests more purpose and organization than "conference," which is vague, and "statutes and cases supporting our position" is more specific and powerful than a general reference to "legal issues."

♦ Use language your client can understand, not technical jargon. If you want your client to understand the value of your services, you have to express that value in terms the client can understand. It may be easy for you to write and understand "preparation of irrevocable life insurance trust with Crummey powers." The client is more likely to understand (and value) "preparation of trust to remove life insurance from taxable estate, with withdrawal rights to qualify the payment of life insurance premiums for the federal gift tax annual exclusion."

♦ Include a description of your services even when billing for a fixed fee. Remember, the purpose of the bill is not merely to justify your fee but to communicate the value of your services. Don't pass up an opportunity to describe the value of your services merely because the amount of the fee has already been determined.

♦ Get it right the first time—when the time is recorded. The easiest way to prepare a bill is for all lawyers, paralegals, and other timekeepers to record their time and the descriptions of their time when the services are rendered and then use an automated time and billing system to pull the time records together and prepare the bill. This only works efficiently if the descriptions of the time and services entered can be printed and presented to the client "as is," without editing or revising. If you want to present the client with descriptions of the value of your services, you and your firm need to enter those descriptions the way you want them when you first enter the time. If you are a solo practitioner or the only timekeeper, you need to learn to think of every time entry as a memo to the client and prepare the descriptions of your time accordingly. If you are a supervising lawyer and have associates and paralegals, you will probably find that they are writing their time descriptions to try to please and impress you or your partners, the ones who sign their paychecks. Therefore, if you want your personnel to write time descriptions designed to please the client, you will have to train them to do it because it will not come naturally to them.

Timing of Bills

A bill is most effective when it follows (or accompanies) a benefit that the client has seen. It is therefore most effective to issue bills after sending the client the documents, recommendations, or other services for which the client is being billed. A corollary of that principle is that, if you bill the same time every month, you should begin reviewing your files at least a week before your regular billing date to ensure that your clients have seen recent results, if possible.

Firms often bill once a month, at the beginning of the month. Many individuals and businesses, however, pay bills at the beginning of the month, so if you send a bill on the first of the month, it will probably not get paid for another thirty days, until the beginning of the following month. If you send out bills in the middle of the month (between the fifteenth and the twentieth), there is a good chance that your bill will be paid within fifteen days, at the beginning of the next month. You might therefore be able to reduce your receivables cycle by half and improve your cash flow simply by billing in the middle of the month.

Lastly, bill as often as possible. A series of small bills is almost always more palatable for the client than one large bill. Fight the urge to let a bill go unsent because of concerns about whether the client will be happy with the bill. If a client is going to be unhappy, it is better to know sooner rather than later. The sooner you find out if the client is going to be unhappy, the sooner you can stop wasting your time working for the client. Better to send the bill and get fired right away than not to bill the client, continue to spend time on the client, and then get fired.

Fiduciary Compensation and Liabilities

Traditionally, estates and trusts lawyers have yearned to be appointed as executors and trustees. As a fiduciary (and not merely counsel to a fiduciary), a lawyer can earn a fee that is not limited by the lawyer's time spent but that may be based on a percentage of income or principal. In addition, a lawyer who is a fiduciary becomes his own client and is less easily fired. However, being appointed as a fiduciary also means that it is much easier for the beneficiaries to sue the lawyer if something goes wrong—or even if nothing goes wrong. Therefore, while the rewards of being a fiduciary may be higher, the risks are also higher.

In recent years, legal malpractice insurers have become increasingly reluctant to insure lawyers who serve on the boards of directors of corporations, and similar concerns have begun to affect lawyers who serve as executors or trustees. Malpractice carriers have begun looking at the practice of lawyers serving as fiduciaries, and no lawyer should accept such an appointment without checking with his or her insurer to see whether the potential liabilities will be covered or whether steps must be taken to limit the exposure of the lawyer, firm, and insurer.

A related concern is the problem of estate or trust funds lost to employee theft or negligence (discussed in Chapter 7). Every lawyer or law firm that handles funds as a fiduciary or for a fiduciary should have accounting controls in place to be certain that all of the funds can be accounted for and cannot be "diverted" by a dishonest employee.

Communicating with Clients 5

I was gratified to be able to answer promptly, and I did. I said I didn't know.

—Mark Twain,
Life on the Mississippi

COMMUNICATING EFFECTIVELY WITH CLIENTS is important to the client and to you. It is mainly during your communications with your client that your client decides whether he or she is satisfied with your services and you decide whether you are satisfied with your career.

Client Satisfaction

In medicine, the old joke is that the operation was a success but the patient died. In law, a newer joke is that the lawyer wins the lawsuit (or closes the deal) but the client *still* isn't satisfied! How could the client not be satisfied if you followed all the "right" legal steps and achieved the "right" result? Because clients, like lawyers, have needs that go beyond money, property, and business—and those needs often are not met.

Based on bar association surveys of clients, it appears that the most important quality for most clients in selecting a lawyer is not training, experience, or even ethics but whether the lawyer *cares* about the client and the client's problems. This concern about the lawyer's attitude toward the client may sound silly at first, but it is quite logical if you keep in mind that most clients come to lawyers at a time of trouble, with problems to be solved, or in the midst of change or chaos. This is particularly true when clients come to estates lawyers.

Almost all change is stressful, and so are almost all the events for which people need to consult an estates lawyer, be it about a death, birth, illness or incapacity, marriage, new home purchase, or formation of a new business or partnership. A client who comes to a lawyer in one of those stressful situations almost always needs emotional support, the kind of support that lets you know that you are not alone and that someone cares about what happens to you. You don't need to hug your clients or give them money. You do need to care about them and be concerned about what happens to them because that is something they need along with legal advice and representation.

Estates lawyers also become involved in some of the most intimate details of a client's life. Estate planning may require discussing a client's judgments about the intelligence or integrity of the client's spouse and children. Estate administrations require a lawyer to deal with family members at a time of grief and often require a lawyer to understand and resolve family conflicts that arise after death. A client communicating with a lawyer on such personal matters needs assurance that the lawyer hears and understands the client and respects the client's privacy.

Another way to look at the issue of communication and support is to imagine the lawyer as a guide or interpreter helping the client through a strange and sometimes frightening land (the legal system) inhabited by people who speak an unfamiliar language (legalese). If you cannot help your client understand what is happening and what needs to be done and why, then the client must follow your instructions blindly and on pure faith. That may not be comfortable for most clients.

A final consideration is that your clients have no real way of judging your abilities as a lawyer. Most of the time they can't know whether your tax calculations are right or whether the wills and trusts are written properly. They can, though, judge whether they like the way they have been treated and whether they like what they see of your writings to them and your behavior when you are with them. Thus, clients may judge you less for *what* you say and what you do than for *how* you say and do it.

For other ideas on client satisfaction, see *Through the Client's Eyes: New Approaches to Get Clients to Hire You Again and Again,* by Henry W. Ewalt, published by the ABA Law Practice Management Section.

Lawyer Satisfaction

If you want further incentives to work on your communications skills, consider that your own professional satisfaction may be dependent on your clients' satisfaction. In other words, how happy you are in your career may be directly related to how happy your clients are with your services and how much respect you receive from them.

Oral Communications: How to Listen

Listening is integral to what we do as lawyers, but it is also a large part of client satisfaction and lawyer satisfaction. How do you create satisfied clients? I suggest two steps:

1. Get yourself out of the way.
2. Actively listen to the client.

Get Yourself Out of the Way

Before you can listen to your client, you have to get yourself out of your own way. You should get rid of any fear or anger you might have, and you should set aside your own agenda of what you think about the client or yourself. You need to respect and care about your client.

Eliminating Fear and Anger

It is easy to see how we might fear an angry client, but fear can arise in subtle ways with even mild-mannered or friendly clients. If you have ever met with a client and found yourself worrying about whether the client will hire you and trust you—or whether you really know what you are doing—then you have experienced fear. Anger is similar to fear and can arise when you are frustrated with the client's inability to understand your explanations, or when you are simply in a bad mood.

While a lawyer's fear or anger can make it more difficult for the lawyer to hear the client, it may also make it more difficult for the client to hear the lawyer. A lawyer's fear may be sensed by the client and can make the client fearful and unable to listen as well. Moreover, few of us—including clients—like to associate with people who are unhappy, depressed, angry, or troubled. The client may therefore not want to listen to a lawyer who the client feels is unhappy.

Eliminating fear, anger, and other negative emotions is the subject of entire books, and the problem can't be solved here. If, however, you are aware of the problem, you may be able to overcome it simply through your awareness. If not, you may wish to consult a book like *Living with the Law—Strategies to Avoid Burnout and Create Balance,* edited by Julie M. Tamminen and published by the ABA Law Practice Management Section.

Discarding Your Agenda

Even if you are able to get your emotional baggage out of the way, you still need to get rid of your mental and intellectual baggage before you can really listen to a client. In meeting with and communicating with a client, we are often impeded (based on the same Latin roots as *impedimenta,* meaning "baggage") by our attitudes and preconceptions. We are so busy jumping to conclusions that we stop listening.

A client presents us with a particular problem and we begin to make assumptions about what happened or what the client wants before the client is finished talking. Perhaps the lawyer sees the client as elderly and starts making assumptions about what elderly people want and how they want to be treated. Another lawyer sees that the client is dressed simply and cheaply and assumes that the client is poor or uneducated. If the client is well-dressed, the lawyer assumes that the client is most concerned with achieving the best financial result, regardless of moral or emotional issues.

A worse problem is when we let our own ambitions or agendas influence how we view the client. We want to earn a fee, so we want the client to have the type of problem that will earn us a fee. We want the client to think that we are smart, so we start trying to impress the client with our knowledge of the law by telling the client the answer before the client is finished with the question.

A common disservice to our clients is that we concentrate on tax planning and give too little weight to the client's personal preferences. We let the tax planning tail wag the estate planning dog. For example, many estate planners believe that a good way to save income taxes is to make the unified credit or family trust a "sprinkle" or "spray" trust so that the trustee can distribute income to either the surviving spouse or the children, as needed, and so be able to move taxable income into the (possibly) lower income tax brackets of the children. However, when I meet with new clients to review their old wills and those wills include sprinkle provisions, most of those clients want to change the documents to give the surviving spouse *all* of the income once I have explained what it means to give that power to the trustee. The possible income tax saving simply isn't as important as the financial security and independence of the surviving husband or wife. Many estate planners lead clients into estate plans that are more complicated or restrictive than the client wants because the estate planner believes that the tax savings are more important than the client's wishes.

Respecting the Client

Once you have learned to discard your fears about the client and your preconceptions about who the client is and what the client wants, you should be able to see the client for who the client really is and give the client the respect and honest concern that the client wants.

Respect in this context means a willingness to treat the client as a responsible human being entitled to make his or her own decisions. The belief that we know better than our clients is a patronizing and demeaning point of view that can only interfere with the relationship with the client. We should always make sure that clients understand the meaning and possible consequences of their decisions. We should discourage clients from making decisions based on fear or anger, but there is a certain point at which we must accept the client's decisions and either help the client carry them out or get out of the client's way so that he or she can find a lawyer who will.

Listen Actively to Your Client

Listening is more than not talking. If you keep quiet and nod your head while your client rambles on and on, you are not listening, and your client will probably know it.

If you have gotten yourself out of the way and are truly concerned about the client, you will almost have to listen to the client. There are ways to communicate to the client that you are listening and to assure the client that you have heard and understand what he or she has said. One technique is what I call "simple mirroring," in which you repeat or paraphrase key elements of the client's story to confirm that you have heard what the client is saying. An important element in mirroring is "validation," which means that you confirm that the client's point of view and emotional response to the situation (whether fear, anger, or anxiety) are normal and understandable under the circumstances. Validation does not mean that you accept the client's version of the situation as true and accurate or ratify the decisions that the client has made, only that you let clients know that their point of view is understandable and that you consider them to be sane and rational.

Mirroring and other techniques for successful client communications are described in more detail in *Connecting with Your Client: Success through Improved Client Communication Techniques,* by Noelle C. Nelson, Ph.D., published by the ABA Law Practice Management Section.

Needless to say, these techniques can also be used to convince a client that you are concerned about the client and care about the client's problems when you actually do not care. This manipulative behavior probably won't work for very long, though, and is not recommended.

A great deal of client satisfaction comes from the belief that the lawyer has heard the client's point of view and cares about the client. If you can overcome your fears and preconceptions and care for the client, you will be able to listen to the client. If you can listen to the client, the client will be happy with you and your work. What could be better than that?

What We Communicate

As a lawyer, you will of course explain the law to the client, as well as your recommendations. Is there anything else that needs to be communicated to the client?

Give the Client a Road Map

What constitutes an emergency for the average person is a matter of routine for the expert. What is to you a frightening injury is to a doctor just another fracture that needs to be set and put in a cast. You must always remember that your clients don't know what you know. They don't see their legal problems as calmly as you do. That is why you always need to explain what is happening. Give the client a simple road map of where you're going.

When first meeting with a client and from time to time in later meetings and correspondence, it is reassuring to explain to (or remind) the client where you are going, why you are going there, and when you expect to get there. For example, a first meeting with the family in an estate administration should include an explanation of what is meant by an estate administration (e.g., collecting the assets, paying the debts and taxes, and distributing the assets) and how long it will take. Similarly, a client who is faced with an estate tax audit will want some idea of what will happen, how long it will take, and what results might be expected.

Set Reasonable Expectations

Most lawyers understand that a client is more likely to be satisfied with a result if the possibilities and difficulties of obtaining a good result are explained in advance. A tax deficiency of $50,000 may be delightful if the client was expecting a deficiency of $100,000, but it is disappointing if the client was expecting not to pay any additional tax. How we view events is more often a product of our expectations than of whether the event is "good" or "bad" in the abstract.

For that reason it is a good idea to set clients' and others' expectations as soon as possible. When communicating with the beneficiaries of an estate (whether your clients or the beneficiaries of an estate for which you represent the executor), you should provide a reasonable after-tax projection of distributions from the estate as soon as you can. Beneficiaries often have an inflated idea of the estate's value and fail to take into account debts, expenses, taxes, or the shares of other beneficiaries in estimating their own shares. Giving them the bad news (or the good news) within the first few months is better than letting them wait a year or two before being disappointed.

Establish Clear Obligations and Deadlines

While clients like to know *what* is happening, they also like to know *when* things will happen. If you are not specific about when something will be done, a misunderstanding may arise between you and the client about when to expect action and the client may be disappointed or upset when nothing happens at the time the client expects. For example, if you say that you will research a question and write to the client with the answer, the client may become apprehensive, not knowing when to expect your response or maybe expecting it in two or three days when you had planned to take a week or more. It is better to set a clear timetable than to leave open the possibility of misunderstandings. Of course, once you set a clear schedule, you have to keep it to maintain client confidence.

The steps to be taken and the responsibility for those steps must be clear at all times. Several guidelines will be helpful in keeping your obligations clear.

First, be specific about your responsibilities and your services. Chapter 4 suggests that fee agreements be as clear as possible about what services are and are not included in the agreement. Similarly, your communications with your clients should always be clear about what you are and are not doing. Don't simply tell your client that you will proceed with the "administration of the estate." Explain that you will be preparing the documents for the probate of the will and collecting asset information to prepare for the death tax returns that are due in nine months. If you are not planning to do anything about collecting the life insurance proceeds or retirement plan benefits, both of which are payable directly to the client and are not part of the probate estate, then say so. Whatever you do, don't allow the client to be confused about what you are doing, and don't allow the client to assume that you are responsible for doing things that you don't intend to do.

Second, don't let any meeting end without a clear agreement about what happens next. Otherwise, you may walk out of a meeting with clients or other lawyers and then realize when you get back to your office that you aren't sure what you are supposed to do next. The last thing to do at any client meeting is to look the client straight in the eyes and say either, "So it's agreed that I will draft the documents we have discussed today and send them to you within the next two weeks," or, "So you still need to give me the names of the trustees you want to appoint, and I will wait for those names from you before doing anything further." In other words, clearly and unambiguously declare the next step to be taken and the person responsible for taking that step. It must be the last thing discussed, or it will be lost, forgotten, or misunderstood. Look the client in the eyes to make sure that the client hears and understands and that there is a real agreement. Otherwise, the client sits at home waiting for the documents while you sit at the office waiting for the client to call with the names you need.

Third, end every letter to your client with a clear statement of what still needs to be done. This is similar but a bit broader than the preceding guideline about agreements at the end of meetings. After a client meeting, you will often have a list of things to do, some of which are due immediately and some of which are longer-term projects to be completed later. When you next write to the client, sending answers to questions or drafts of documents, you state what the client needs to do next (e.g., call me, sign the documents, or send me other information) and what you need to do next. Thus, the next step of the process is clear. You should also include a summary of the other matters discussed at the meeting, even if you have done nothing on them and don't expect to do anything in the near future. The letter serves as a confirmation and reminder of everything that was discussed, and it covers the entire plan of action for the client.

Furthermore, as you send additional documents or advice to the client, completing each project in the plan, end each letter with a reminder of both what has now been completed and what is not yet completed. In other words, use almost every letter to remind the client of all the things that are not yet done. The first advantage of this procedure is that you are maintaining a checklist of things to do that is updated with each letter to the client. Each letter becomes an opportunity to review what you have done and where you are going. In addition, because each letter is a complete list of things to do, you need only look at the last letter to the client to review the file's status.

The other advantage is that the client is continually reminded of what else needs to be done. This reassures the client and protects you. The client is comforted with the assurance that you still remember everything that was discussed and that it will all be completed in the order discussed. You are continually reassured that the client has not forgotten your decisions and that nothing has occurred to change your plans. When you finally complete the last of the things you said you would do, the client should not be surprised by what you did and should not complain about the necessity or value of your services.

Here are a couple of corollaries to the importance of meeting deadlines and fulfilling obligations to your clients in a timely way:

- ◆ Return phone calls as promptly as possible. Clients always expect calls to be returned promptly, so that is the expectation you must live with.
- ◆ It is better to respond promptly than to respond completely. If the client expects a response by a certain date and you don't have the full answer, tell the client what you have learned to date and when you will have the complete answer. The principle is that it is better to keep your word to your client about the date of your response than to ignore the obligation completely. Of course, this only works once or twice. If you don't have the answer by the third deadline, the client will realize that you have trouble setting—and meeting—realistic deadlines.

Know That the Client Is Always Right

We've all heard the expression, "The customer is always right." Well, the client is always right, but it took me several years to figure out why and how.

The client is always right because we are in a service industry, which means that our primary product is client satisfaction. The client knows whether or not he or she is satisfied. If the client is not satisfied and complains, we have not done our job. In that sense, the client is always right because the client is always right to complain if her or his expectations have not been met.

That the client is right does not mean that the client is not confused or mistaken, only that you have failed to educate or guide the client properly. One memorable experience I had as an associate was to send some documents to a client for a signature. At the instructions of the senior lawyer, the signature lines had the client's name typed underneath and the client's initials penciled in, removable sticky-notes pointed to the lines for the client's signature, and paper clips were positioned on the signature pages opposite the signature lines. I tried to point out to the senior lawyer that this was overkill, perhaps even insulting, because the client was a business executive and should be able to find the right line on which to sign. The senior lawyer insisted, so I did as I was told, and of course the documents came back with the signatures on the wrong lines. It was then my job to call the client and apologize for the misunderstanding because our instructions weren't clear enough.

There are no ignorant clients, only clumsy lawyers. Communicating to your clients that they are right—and that you know it—is a key part of client satisfaction.

Client Meetings

Two key types of client meetings are the estate planning client interview and the meeting with the executors or family at the beginning of an estate administration. The general principles previously discussed can be illustrated by some specific suggestions for these meetings.

Estate Planning Interviews

Estate planning can be thought of as a rainbow or a spectrum. At one end, taxes are absolutely minimized, both during the client's lifetime and for generations of descendants to come. Yet to achieve that result through a combination of lifetime gifts, generation-skipping trusts, and other arrangements, the client will have to surrender almost all control over his or her financial affairs during his or her lifetime, and the client's children will similarly have little or no control over their inheritances, which will be invested and distributed by trustees for several generations. At the other end of the spectrum, the client and the client's spouse can retain ownership and control of all assets during their lifetimes and transfer total ownership to their children. This end of the spectrum usually results in the greatest possible tax. Most clients find a comfortable balance somewhere in the middle of the spectrum, where they give up some control and save some taxes. How do you help the client find that comfort zone?

An estate planning conference can start from either end of the estate planning spectrum:

1. You can start by obtaining asset and family information and developing a tax-oriented set of estate planning recommendations, showing a range of actions and the tax savings that should result, then discuss the recommendations with the client to determine whether the tax recommendations suit the client's personal preferences; or
2. You can start by asking the client what he or she (or they) want to achieve and their ideas, desires, and goals, then introduce tax planning techniques that are consistent with those goals (as well as a few extra, just to make sure that the client has a full range of choices).

The direction to start from may depend on the client. Some clients have definite ideas about what they want, and they want to explain their goals and get answers to their questions. In those cases, it is usually better to let the clients talk, learn about them, and help them understand the advantages and disadvantages of what they want to do. Other clients have no definite ideas (beyond, perhaps, saving taxes) and welcome the estate planner's questions and direction.

In either case, a typical estate planning interview will probably include a brief explanation of estates in general. Clients talking about estate planning for the first time may be embarrassed by how little they know about wills, trusts, probate, and death taxes. The best antidote to those feelings is a brief explanation of what a will does, how probate works, and what taxes must be considered. The exact form and content of the explanation will depend on the client's needs and experience, but it should at least touch on the following factors:

- ◆ The function of a will in disposing of property at death and what happens after death (probate, payment of debts and death taxes, and distribution by the executor).
- ◆ The disposition of property passing outside of a will, such as life insurance, retirement benefits, and property held as joint tenants with right of survivorship.
- ◆ Other possible functions of a will, such as the appointment of guardians for minors and anatomical gifts.
- ◆ The function and purpose of revocable inter vivos trusts (if appropriate to the state and the client).

Most clients will want some explanation of the federal estate tax system, and any state death tax, which explanation will usually include the following information:

- ◆ The assets that are subject to federal estate tax. Many clients are surprised to learn that life insurance, retirement benefits, jointly owned property, and revocable trusts are subject to estate tax.
- ◆ The federal estate tax unified credit, which can usually be described as an exclusion or "zero bracket amount" for the federal estate tax.
- ◆ The progressive rates applicable to the federal estate tax. Most clients are surprised to hear that once the unified credit exclusion amount is exceeded, the tax rates begin at 37 percent or more.
- ◆ The marital deduction if the client is married and the charitable deduction if the client has charitable interests.
- ◆ Similar explanations for the scope, exclusions, deductions, and rates for any state death tax.

The estate planning interview should also address tax planning recommendations for the client. These might be prepared and printed in advance if you can obtain asset information from the client in advance. (See Appendix D for a sample form that could be used to request information in advance.)

The personal planning recommendations or considerations for the client also need to be discussed. These can include the following issues:

- The choices for executors and trustees.
- Whether the marital deduction should be an outright distribution or in trust. This is often a delicate discussion when meeting with a husband and wife, since it often turns on each spouse's view of the trustworthiness of the other.
- Whether the inheritances of the children or other beneficiaries should be outright or in trust (even absent any generation-skipping tax considerations).
- Discussions of durable powers of attorney and advance health care declarations (i.e., living wills).

It is important to keep accurate notes of these meetings, both to fulfill the obligation to the client to carry out the client's wishes as accurately as possible and to protect the estate planner from possible litigation. Many states now allow disappointed heirs to sue estate planning lawyers for malpractice in the preparation of a will or estate plan if the estate plan incurs unnecessary taxes or otherwise gives the beneficiary less than what the client intended. Accurate notes of client meetings and conversations may therefore be needed to show that the result of the estate plan is what the client truly intended.

Various forms may be helpful in obtaining the needed information and recording the client's decisions. The sample questionnaire in Appendix D can be used as a checklist for questions during the meeting and to record the personal and asset information given by the client during the meeting. It might also be convenient to have a checklist of drafting instructions, such as the sample one in Appendix E, to help record the decisions made during the meeting.

The Reading of the Will

The classic "reading of the will" is a scene in many murder mysteries, but it rarely happens in real life. It's much easier to mail photocopies of the will to everyone interested. There is, though, usually a first meeting with the executor (or executors or administrators) and perhaps also the primary beneficiaries to review what needs to be done for the administration and distribution of the estate.

Chapter 7 discusses the advantages of developing a comprehensive plan for an estate administration. The first meeting with the executors and beneficiaries is a good time to start developing that plan. It is also a good time to begin educating the clients and any other attendees about the administration process and what to expect, both in terms of the timing and the amounts of distributions. A good first meeting will include the following:

- ◆ A general review of the estate administration process (collection of assets, payment of debts and taxes, and distribution).
- ◆ A more specific discussion of the probate procedures, such as what papers must be prepared, what notices must be given, who must appear before the relevant officials, and how long it may take.
- ◆ A review of the known assets and debts of the estate and estimates of value.
- ◆ A review of any assets passing outside of the will, such as life insurance, retirement benefits, and jointly owned property, both for estate tax reporting purposes and discussion of what might need to be done in the way of applications for benefits or elections regarding the form or timing of distributions.
- ◆ A brief overview of the provisions of the will or revocable trust and how the federal estate tax applies to those provisions and the estate assets, such as any charitable gifts, unified credit trust, marital-deduction gift or trust, election under Section 6166, or alternate valuation election. These explanations could be helped by a diagram or chart of the division or distribution of the estate.

◆ A discussion of legal fees, if not already agreed on.
◆ A tentative estimate of the expenses of administration, the federal estate tax liability if any, and state death tax liability if any.
◆ A tentative plan for the payment of the taxes and sale of assets needed to pay the debts, expenses, and taxes.
◆ A tentative plan for distribution of the specific gifts (e.g., tangible personal property), any cash gifts, and the residuary estate, including the timing of distributions and the form of distribution.

Although the complexity of an estate, or a lack of information about assets or debts, may limit many of these discussions, it is often possible to walk out of a meeting such as this with a good plan for the administration of an estate. And this is before the will has been probated! Needless to say, clients who go into a meeting about the estate of a recently deceased spouse or parent, feeling not only grief but confusion and fear of the unknown, can be pleased to come out with a much clearer idea of what needs to be done, when it will be done, and what the ultimate result is likely to be.

The results of a meeting like this should be confirmed by letter as soon as possible, both to avoid possible misunderstandings and to emphasize the tentative nature of the projections and estimates. If any plans developed at the meeting need to be changed because of new information or new considerations, all interested parties should be notified as soon as possible.

Written Communications: Letters and Memos

Having talked about oral communications, why we communicate and what we communicate, it is time to talk about the mechanics of how to communicate to your clients in written letters and memos.

Write in English, Not Latin or Legalese

Everyone who writes about legal writing will tell you to write in plain English, yet lawyers usually find it difficult to do so. Lawyers use legal terms and classifications to organize their thinking and to communicate with each other economically and efficiently. Using legal terminology therefore becomes a habit. So, it is much easier to drift into the specialized jargon of law than to make the effort to explain what you really need to say.

The most effective way to avoid legalese is to write about what is going to happen from the client's point of view. For example, if you write to the client, "Your will needs to establish a spousal bypass trust in order to use your federal estate tax unified credit," you will have said something clear and intelligible to another lawyer—but gibberish to the client. If you think about what the recommendation means from the client's point of view, you can write, "After your death, the part of your estate that is free from federal estate tax because of the unified credit needs to be set up as a separate account from which your wife can receive the income, but with only limited powers to withdraw from the account, so that the account will not be taxed at her death and your children can then receive the money free of tax."

You will still have to explain about trusts and trustees and how much is free of tax and why, but the second letter provides a much clearer statement of the important facts from the client's point of view. It underscores that we are talking about what will happen after his death, not during his lifetime; that his wife will have limited rights in part of his assets, which will be held in some sort of separate account; and that the arrangement will save taxes for his children, but not for him or his wife.

Like many other professionals, lawyers often think that they have explained something when all they have done is put a different label on it. If you think about communications with your clients as a matter of explaining the practical effects of decisions rather than merely applying legal labels to things, you will find it much easier to avoid the legalese that confuses so many people.

Write Like It's an Army Field Manual

One of the most valuable pieces of advice I got in law school was to write in the form of an army field manual. Of course, my writing instructor was talking about how to communicate with judges and senior partners and other persons with limited attention spans, not clients, but I have never had a client complain because my letters were too clear or too understandable.

For those who don't know, army field manuals are written at about the eighth-grade level, which the army hopes is understandable to its average soldier. Field manuals have an interesting and easy-to-follow writing style that can be summarized like this:

1. Tell them what you're going to tell them.
2. Tell them.
3. Then tell them what you told them.

This formula might seem to lead to unnecessary repetition, but it does not if you handle it correctly. You will be amazed at how easy and natural it is to compose a multipage letter beginning with, "I am writing to explain the benefits of the new tax law," then continue with "The benefits of the new tax law include the following. . .," and conclude with "I hope that you will see the benefits of the new tax law to you and will take the steps that I have recommended." The beginning of the letter sets the stage, letting the client know why you are writing, what the letter is about, and why the client should read it. The body of the letter tells the client what you want the client to know. The conclusion is a summary to confirm and reinforce the point of the letter and to remind the client of what the client needs to do (if anything).

Determine the Purpose of Your Letter

If you tell clients what you're going to tell them, then you tell them, and then you tell them what you told them, you have written a letter that clearly tells them something. Still, you have to ask yourself, why? Why am I writing this letter to the client? What result do I hope to achieve? Is this letter the best way to achieve that result? A basic test for any letter is to read it to yourself before it is mailed and ask two questions:

1. What result do I want from this letter?
2. Am I likely to get that result?

If you can't answer the first question, or the answer to the second question is no, you have some rethinking and rewriting to do.

Deciding that your clients need the information you are sending them is not good enough. Why do they need the information? What do you expect them to do with the information? Do you really think that the clients want the information? There is a big difference between writing a letter to a client to make certain disclosures required by law or to protect yourself against a possible malpractice action and writing a letter to the client with information that the client needs to know and will want to act on. If you don't have that kind of distinction clearly in your mind when you write the letter, you are going to confuse the client. And a confused client is usually not a happy client.

Every letter that you write should have a clear purpose, a clear result you want to achieve. The purpose might be merely to impress the client with your knowledge of the newest tax laws, to encourage the client to take some specific action, or simply to keep the client informed of the progress of the estate administration (or whatever the representation might be). In any event, once you decide on the letter's purpose, what you write should be devoted to that purpose. Don't write a letter that starts out with a status report and then suddenly tells the client that a decision is needed. Similarly, don't write a letter that tells the client that some kind of decision is needed but that is vague about what the decision might be or when it needs to be made. Such mixed messages or indecisiveness will drive your clients crazy.

Use Headings and Lists

Another way to make a long letter easier to read and understand is to break it into shorter sections with section headings. For example, a letter about a new tax law, how it affects the client, and what the client needs to do could be broken into three sections: "The New Law," "What It Means to You," and "What to Do Next." It sounds corny, but it is effective because the section headings act like road signs, letting us know what's ahead.

Who among us has not opened a letter from another lawyer, found two or three pages of solid single-spaced text, and not felt a touch of despair in having to wade through the letter to find out what it's about? Take pity on your clients and give them some signs to see what is coming in your letters so that they are not like the children in a car whining, "When do we get there?" Your clients will appreciate knowing where they are going and how long it will take to get there—and as a result may actually look forward to reading your letters and then getting there.

Another aid to clear writing is to use numbered, bulleted, or indented lists. For example, if there are five things that the client needs to do, put the five things into a list, numbered one through five, so the client can clearly see that these are the things that he or she needs to do and in what order they need to be done.

Write to the Client, Not at the Client

The client should believe that the letter or memo is a personal communication from you to the client, not an abstract explanation or article. The letter should sound and feel like you talking to the client in your office, not like a speech in a large hall.

The difference is in the level of the client's interest. Your clients must care about what you think or they would not have hired you. When they read your letters, they want to hear what you have to say and to "hear" it in your words and in your voice. A client will be more interested in a letter that is clearly written for him or her and with him or her in mind. A well-written letter should convey to the reader a sense of urgency, a personal appeal to hear and understand what the writer has to say.

Don't underestimate the difficulty of this. In *The Shock of the New,* art critic Robert Hughes wrote that all great art is fundamentally a communication between two people, the artist and the individual viewer. A viewer of great art feels a personal communication from the artist in which the artist shares with the viewer a personal and intimate view of how the artist sees the world. I am suggesting to you that your letters to your clients should be more than merely legally correct—they should be works of art, conveying your personal view of the law to your client.

The best way to test for the voice of the letter is to read it out loud. If the language or phrasings don't feel natural, try rewriting the letter so that it sounds more like the way you talk.

Numbers and Charts in Presentations

In striving for clarity and understanding in your client presentations, consider using specific numbers to illustrate estate planning concepts and recommendations. In explaining estate and trust administrations, using graphs and charts helps explain estates and trusts in a visual way.

For many people, understanding tax concepts in the abstract is very difficult. Even experienced lawyers can have difficulty understanding the impact of a particular tax without a specific example. Without specific examples and projections, it is also easy to make bad assumptions about the cost of a particular tax or the savings from a tax planning technique. Without testing the principles by performing an actual calculation, you may make a recommendation to a client that will cost the client additional taxes instead of saving taxes. It is therefore extremely useful to illustrate tax planning recommendations with specific numbers.

Specific numbers may also help the client appreciate the value of the lawyer's services. The client may not know how much faith to put in your assertion that your recommendations will "save taxes," but the client may be very impressed and grateful to receive projections that show that your estate planning recommendations may help the client's children save $200,000 or more in taxes. See Figure 1 for a comparison of tax consequences for a hypothetical tax planning decision.

Numbers may be too abstract or difficult to grasp for many clients, which is why graphs and charts can be more effective. You might, for example, advise the client that his or her estate will continue to grow in value and that lifetime giving will help reduce the percentage of the estate to be paid in taxes. You might even produce numbers to illustrate what you are recommending, but the client may still have trouble understanding the impact of future growth and lifetime gifts. However, if you present a line graph that shows the estate growing along with an ever-growing tax liability and an ever-shrinking share of the estate for the children contrasted with a graph in which the shares of the children grow without the same growth in taxes, the visual effect may be more persuasive than either your numbers or your words. See Figure 2 for an example of a line graph that illustrates tax savings using the federal gift tax annual exclusion. A pie chart can also help show the impact of taxes, and the pie chart in Figure 3 shows the taxes payable from a qualified retirement plan following the death of the employee.

FIGURE 1

Effect of Disclaimer by Surviving Spouse

	Present Will	Partial Disclaimer	Total Disclaimer
Adjusted Gross Estate	3,592,200	3,592,200	3,592,200
Marital Deduction	2,967,200	1,092,200	0
Taxable Estate	625,000	2,500,000	3,592,200
Pa. Inheritance Tax	93,750	375,000	538,830
Federal Estate Tax	0	684,950	1,176,409
Total Taxes	93,750	1,059,950	1,715,239
Distribution of Estate			
Marital Trust	2,967,200	1,092,200	0
Nonmarital Trust	531,250	1,440,050	1,876,961
Net (After Taxes)	3,498,450	2,532,250	1,876,961
Survivor's Estate			
Survivor's Assets	16,000,000	16,000,000	16,000,000
Marital Trust (Taxable)	2,967,200	1,092,200	0
Taxable Estate	18,967,200	17,092,200	16,000,000
Pa. Inheritance Tax	2,845,080	2,563,830	2,400,000
Federal Estate Tax	7,817,518	6,992,518	6,511,950
Death Taxes	10,662,598	9,556,348	8,911,950
Total Taxes (Both Estates)			
Pa. Inheritance Tax	2,938,830	2,938,830	2,938,830
Federal Estate Tax	7,817,518	7,677,468	7,688,359
Combined Death Taxes	10,756,348	10,616,298	10,627,189
Tax Savings		140,050	129,159

FIGURE 2

Tax Consequences of Annual Gifts
$3 Million Estate; 4% Annual Growth

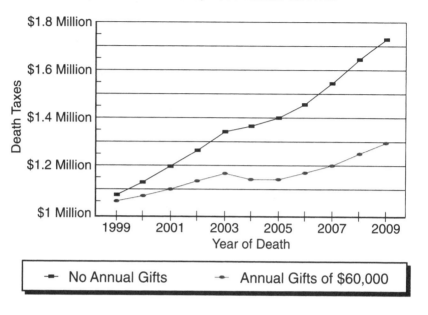

FIGURE 3

Retirement Plan Taxation

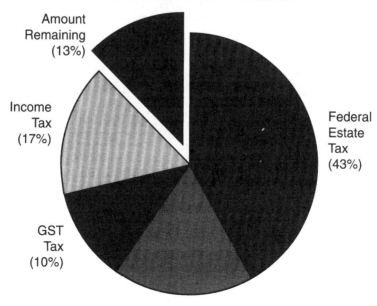

Likewise, clients often have difficulty understanding how an estate is divided and what shares of the estate go to what trust, whether marital deduction or unified credit. A flow chart that shows the different assets of the estate and how they are divided can help the client understand the different parts of the estate plan and how they work together. Figure 4 is a flow chart of an estate plan with tax projections included.

Fortunately, computer programs are available to help you prepare such numeric illustrations, graphs, and charts. This kind of software is discussed in detail in my book *Wills, Trusts, and Technology: An Estate Lawyer's Guide to Automation,* published jointly by the ABA Real Property, Probate and Trust Law Section and Law Practice Management Section. I also discussed some of the most current software in my column in *Probate & Property,* March/April 1998.

FIGURE 4

John and Mary Client
Plan 2 - John's credit used for bypass trust; Balance to Mary outright

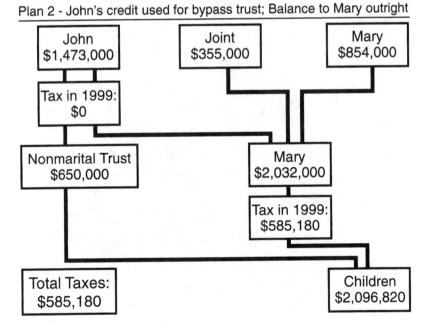

Forms for Clients

Although communications with clients should be personal in the sense that the client should be able to feel the lawyer's interest in the client's affairs, forms such as preprinted letters, guidelines, instructions, and checklists do have their place in communicating with clients.

Advantages of Forms

Preprinted (or automated) checklists and forms can serve a number of different goals:

- ◆ Forms save time. We obviously don't want to spend time reinventing the wheel, and we shouldn't have to spend time rewriting the same explanations or instructions for multiple clients. Having standard sets of explanations, instructions, and other forms can dramatically reduce the time needed to communicate with clients.
- ◆ Forms reduce errors and omissions. Having a prepared explanation or instruction reduces the chance of leaving something out or otherwise making a mistake. Over time, the forms can be improved and refined, reducing the number of mistakes that might be made if the explanation or instruction had to be prepared from scratch each time.
- ◆ Forms can reassure the client. Although preprinted forms may seem impersonal, they carry other messages that the client may find reassuring. For example, the fact that you have a standard form for a particular transaction means that you have done it before, so it confirms your experience. A standard checklist or guideline also assures the client that you are thorough and that nothing will be overlooked or forgotten. In short, personal attention is important and reassuring, but it is also reassuring for the client to know that there is a routine and that the client can safely follow the routine recommended by the lawyer.

Types of Forms

The following types of prepared forms can be helpful in an estates practice:

- ◆ A checklist or questionnaire of the personal and asset information needed for estate planning purposes. (See Appendix D.)
- ◆ Execution instructions for clients executing wills, trusts, powers of attorney, or other documents outside of the office and without a lawyer present. (See Appendix I for an example of a form for will execution instructions.)
- ◆ Instructions for completing and submitting an application for an employer identification number for an estate or trust, particularly if the application can be made by telephone.
- ◆ Instructions for the administration of irrevocable life insurance trusts or other "Crummey" trusts.
- ◆ A checklist or questionnaire of information about the decedent and the beneficiaries that will be needed for an estate administration. (See Appendix F.)
- ◆ A checklist of the information needed about the assets and liabilities of the estate, particularly the exact information needed for federal estate tax purposes. (See Appendix G.) This type of form is especially useful if the executor has assumed responsibility for collecting the information needed by the lawyer for various tax returns.
- ◆ A timeline or checklist of the various steps needed for the administration of the estate, so that the executors (and beneficiaries) will have an idea in advance of the steps that must be taken, when they must be completed, and how long the estate administration may require. (See Appendix H.)
- ◆ Summaries of laws or considerations that clients may wish to consider in advance of meetings for particular purposes, such as a summary of the laws relating to prenuptial agreements or shareholder agreements, with possible approaches or options to be considered by the people considering those agreements.

◆ Any other type of summary, explanation, instruction, check-list, or guidelines that you believe might be useful in your practice or might be appreciated by your clients.

Miscellaneous Tips on Client Communications

Finally, here are a few other tips and observations on client communications and relations.

◆ Don't be afraid to say that you don't know. If a question comes up during a meeting or phone conversation with a client and you aren't sure of the answer, say so, but also tell the client when (or whether) you will find out the answer. Any other response is foolish because you are not being honest with the client and the client will eventually figure that out. If the client can't accept the fact that you don't know everything, the client has some unreasonable expectations that need to be corrected sooner rather than later.

◆ Deliver bad news as soon as possible. When things don't go according to plan, tell the client as soon as possible. The longer you let bad news fester, the longer the client lives with the wrong information, and the worse the client's reaction may be when the truth is finally told. Also, if the client is going to fire you, you might as well find out as soon as possible, before spending more time for which you may not get paid.

◆ Never tell the client "no" without also providing an alternative. Lawyers have a reputation as deal killers because they always seem to be looking for problems, not solutions. If a client asks about a particular transaction or action and it isn't legal or won't work, don't just say "no." Instead, offer the client some possible solution or positive advice that might fit the client's needs. For example, if a client asks if she could save taxes by transferring bonds to her children while retaining the right to the income from the bonds, you would have to explain that the gift couldn't save any death taxes. However, you could also explain the principles of a GRAT to see if that might serve the same purpose.

◆ Send clients copies of everything you receive and everything you send out. There are several advantages to sending the client *everything*, regardless of whether the client needs or will understand it. It assures the client that some progress is being made. It assures the client that there are no secret communications or documents hidden from the client. It shows the client the volume of activity that has taken place, which may help the client to see the reasonableness of the fee that will be paid. It also is easier to send clients everything than to pick and choose and run the risk of not sending something important.

Managing Files and Information

6

All actions and reactions can only increase the chaos and disorder in the universe.

—The Second Law of
Thermodynamics

MOST OF WHAT LAWYERS DO involves the management of information and documents. Client information, along with judgments about the law and personal choices, is converted into wills and trusts and the other documents that make up the client's estate plan. After the client's death, the will is probated and asset information is collected and converted into an estate tax return. Even a will contest can be viewed as the lawyer taking the witnesses' memories and testimonies, arranging them in a logical and persuasive order, and presenting them to the court along with information about the relevant statutes and precedents that the court needs to decide the case.

This chapter provides some suggestions for managing the information and documents necessary to an estates practice.

Client Information

You obviously want to keep track of your clients' names and addresses. There are several reasons why that information should be automated for easy access:

- Client mailings, such as announcements, newsletters, and holiday greeting cards, are much easier to send if you have a database of client information.
- Law firms need a central database of client information to avoid conflicts of interest. You don't want one of your partners to be suing one of your clients, do you?
- You can serve your clients faster and more efficiently if you have basic information about the client readily accessible.

There are even better reasons to take information automation beyond a "computerized Rolodex." In matters on which you're currently working, you can include such things as lists of the tasks to be done and a record of what has been done on each matter. This is usually referred to as "case management."

Automated Case Management

Until recently, automated case management has been mainly for litigators, particularly personal injury lawyers with hundreds of active cases who need a system to track filing deadlines for all those cases. Case management has also been a tool of large firms, providing a way to keep track of which lawyers and paralegals are working on which cases, as well as to track potential conflicts of interest and filing deadlines. These days, case management programs are more powerful and useful, and several programs have become general and flexible enough to be useful to an estates and trusts practice regardless of firm size.

This section describes the basic functions of case management software and then explains how this software can help make the work flow in an estates practice more efficient and effective.

Case Management Functions

In general, case management software is designed to track the following kinds of information, and perform the following functions:

- **Names, addresses, and phone numbers:** In its most rudimentary form, case management software can be nothing more than an automated card file. Case management software can also reorganize and apply that information more usefully. For example, a program should be able to organize names by case so that you can see the names, addresses, and phone numbers of all the fiduciaries or beneficiaries involved with a particular estate.

- **Case information:** In addition to the names of parties, litigators have used case management programs to save other types of information about a case, such as the nature of the litigation, critical dates regarding accidents or injuries, the amounts in dispute, the court in which the claim has been filed, and other notes about the issues in the case and the available evidence. Newer, more flexible programs can be modified to save the information needed for an estate planning or estate administration practice, such as the domicile of the client, the size of the estate, the date of the will or codicils, the date of death, and tax issues to be noted (e.g., marital deduction issues or generation-skipping elections to be made).

- **To-do lists:** Keeping track of filing deadlines and other lists of things to do was one of the original purposes of case management software. Besides showing the case, type of task, and due date, programs can assign priorities to tasks and identify the lawyer or staff member responsible for the task. A lawyer can therefore see all of her or his to-do list, sorted by priority, or just the to-do list for a particular client or estate. Although estates lawyers do not have the same concerns about deadlines as litigators, there are often tax and other deadlines in an estates practice in addition to client-imposed deadlines. Case management software can help you keep track of these deadlines and maintain compliance with them.

◆ **Telephone messages and events:** Case management software can be used to record phone messages as well as other notes and events for clients and files.

◆ **Appointments and calendars:** Keeping an appointment calendar on a computer has often seemed to be more trouble than it's worth. Larger firms with networked calendar systems, however, can benefit from the ability to search through calendars of different lawyers to find open times for meetings and can use the software to schedule common resources like meeting rooms. There is also some benefit in software that beeps or otherwise reminds you of appointments during the day. The calendar function becomes more useful when it automatically displays the due dates of tasks from the to-do list, as the newer case management programs can.

◆ **Document generation:** Most case management software can now be used to generate word processing documents so that client names, addresses, or other case information can be used to generate letters and notices, or even more complex documents.

Case Management Integration

If case management software was nothing but a series of different unrelated functions, it probably wouldn't be worth the bother because it would mean that every to-do item, event, phone message, and other case event would have to be typed into the computer just to be printed later in a slightly different form. What makes case management software so useful today is that it can actually help with the flow of work within an office, saving instead of taking time.

The increased usefulness of case management software can be summed up in one word: integration. Case management programs can share information among the different parts of the program, such as the to-do lists, calendars, and case records. When you enter a new task on your to-do list, it also shows up in your calendar for the day it is due and in the status report for that case. Case management programs can also share information with time and billing software as well as with word processing and document assembly software.

Case management programs have also become more intelligent in the sense that they can be programmed to save a set of standard tasks and apply them to a particular type of case. These features aid work flow in four key ways:

1. When you open a new client file, the program can automatically add a series of tasks to your to-do list and set the deadlines for the tasks, based on the type of case and the information entered with the case. For example, you might be able to save the timetable of a typical estate administration so that when you open a new estate administration file, the program knows that the inventory is due six months after the grant of letters and the federal estate tax return is due nine months from death. When you apply this timetable to a new case, all the preprogrammed tasks and due dates are automatically entered into your to-do list and your calendar, so you will automatically be reminded of each filing date as it approaches. (You can delete tasks not needed for a particular estate, such as a federal estate tax return for a small estate.)

2. When you need to prepare a letter, notice, or other document, the software may be able to begin a first draft with a mere click of the mouse. Names, addresses, and other information in the case management software can be exported to Microsoft Windows word processing programs like WordPerfect and Word and automatically inserted into forms to create letters, notices, and other relatively simple documents. The software may also be able to export information to more complex document assembly programs, which can ask for additional information as needed to complete drafts of documents such as wills and trusts.

3. When phone calls are made or received, the case management software can be used to take notes of the phone call and add those notes to case records. The software can also time each call from the time you begin taking notes. That time can be used to create an automatic billing record of the call, including the file to which the time should be billed and the person to whom the call was

made. If a follow-up call or other action is needed as a result of the phone conversation, the software may be able to create a new to-do item with a click of the mouse.

4. When a task is checked off from the to-do list and marked as completed, such as a document being prepared or filed, a letter written, or a phone call made, the program can prompt you to create a time and billing record for the time spent on the task. The program may be able to fill in the client and matter information automatically, and perhaps even add a rough description of the time spent, making it considerably easier for lawyers and paralegals to keep accurate time records.

As these examples illustrate, case management software can make it much easier to keep track of what needs to be done, note what has been done, bill for the time spent, and even help create the documents that need to be created. The software can help you record what you need to record without unnecessary typing.

The increased usefulness of this software makes it something to consider for estates and trusts lawyers, not just litigators, and by solo practitioners and small firms, not just large firms. My experiences as a solo practitioner have convinced me that case management software can be extremely helpful to the individual lawyer in promoting and organizing work flow.

Document Inventories

Before getting into the question of how you manage wills, trusts, and other client documents on file, it might be wise to ask whether it is a good idea to have custody of original documents.

The traditional wisdom has been that by having custody of the original will, you could be certain that the fiduciaries or heirs would have to come to you after your client's death and you would have one last opportunity to offer your services for the administration of the estate. However, many lawyers today believe that keeping custody of original wills is more trouble than it is worth for the following reasons:

◆ Keeping custody of the client's documents may imply a duty to ensure that the documents are kept up-to-date. Under this theory, custody of the documents implies an obligation to maintain them, which means that the client must be notified of any change in the law that might make the document provisions less than optimal in any way. Although I am not aware of any court decision to adopt this idea, this is nevertheless a real concern among many lawyers.

◆ Too many clients move without notifying their lawyers, meaning that you might get stuck with warehousing documents that might or might not still be valid, with no way of knowing because you can't get in touch with the client. Without knowing that the client has revoked the document (or has died), you can't risk discarding what might still be a valid document, so you are obliged to continue to provide storage space for documents that may be invalid or obsolete.

◆ Having an opportunity to talk with the fiduciaries or heirs after the client's death isn't much of a benefit. If you have had no previous contact with them, the fact that you get a call from them asking about the location of the will is not going to be much of a foundation for a lawyer-client relationship. As explained elsewhere, administering estates is no longer as profitable as it used to be, in part because most lawyers can no longer simply charge a percentage of the estate, and also because of the increased price competition among lawyers and the increasing willingness of heirs and fiduciaries to shop around and compare prices for legal services.

Despite these concerns, I am still inclined to keep custody of client documents for the following reasons:

◆ It seems that whenever I send original documents to the client, I eventually get a call from the client asking where they are. I have to explain that I don't know where they are because I sent them to him or her. It is therefore my rather cynical conclusion that, if I have custody of the documents, at least one person will know where they are, even if that one person is not the client.

◆ While it is a negative that clients might move without telling you, you can turn it into a positive by using custody of the documents as an opportunity to contact your clients each year or two to remind them that, according to your records, these are the documents in force and this is where they are located and would the clients please let you know if there are any changes. If your notice comes back from the post office marked "Forwarding Order Expired," you have a chance to try to find the client while the trail is still warm.

Most case management systems don't seem to be able to handle document inventory needs. It is not difficult, however, to use a simple database program to maintain the dates, location, and contents of client documents, making it easier to keep track of the documents in your possession as well as to contact clients with old documents or documents that have not been updated to reflect changes in tax laws.

Organization of Paper Files

Despite advances in document imaging and recurring promises of the "paperless office," most of us still have to keep paper records of our client conversations and correspondence as well as the other documents that go into estate planning and administration. This means that we must organize files with these paper records.

Many books have been written on how to organize files. The fact of the matter is that almost any system will work if it is applied consistently, so most lawyers and firms eventually develop some consistent method of organizing paper files. Estate planning and administration files present some unusual problems, though. The following are some general suggestions for the files of an estates practice, followed by specific organizational suggestions for estate planning and estate administration files.

◆ Use a hierarchical numbering system so that related folders can be kept together. Too many systems use a sequential numbering system, so that if you want to add a new folder of special correspondence, it winds up at the back of the file instead of with the other correspondence at the front. I use a two-level numbering system, the first number showing the general type of folder (correspondence, billing, documents, superseded documents, etc.) and the second designating a specific folder within the general category. For example, I might have one folder marked 4 for all client documents, or I might break them out into 4.1 for the will, 4.2 for the power of attorney, and so forth. The use of the decimal separator is arbitrary, and the folders could be designated 4A, 4B, and so on, or any other system that allows similar folders to be grouped together.

◆ Keep records of oral and written communications in a chronological folder. Most lawyers have a correspondence folder, a memos folder, a notes folder, and so forth. The problem with this arrangement is that your notes of your client meeting may be in one folder while your letter to the client summarizing that meeting is in another folder and your memo to the file of your later phone conversation with the client is in a third. This arrangement is not helpful when trying to reconstruct the history of your communications with the client. I have found that it is more efficient to keep all communications in one folder, so that letters, notes of meetings, and memos are in chronological order. If the folder becomes too bulky, it can be divided between client communications and other communications (and other communications can also be subdivided in some cases).

◆ Create an archive file for folders no longer needed. Although it is usually desirable to keep all of a client's records together, sometimes it just gets too bulky, particularly for a long-term client who has gone through a number of different estate plans over the years. In those cases, it may be better to create an archive or inactive file to hold older correspondence, superseded documents, and other papers no longer currently needed.

◆ Don't be afraid to mix correspondence into other folders. Putting the correspondence into one folder is for convenience. It's not a federal law. You should put correspondence into other folders if it is more logical and convenient to do so. If, for example, you have a separate folder with records of the client's life insurance policies, it might make more sense to put insurance company correspondence about the beneficiary designations into that folder, where it can be found quickly, rather than into the general correspondence folder, where it might take time to find when needed.

Estate Planning Files

As noted, I have found it best to have general groupings of folders, with subfolders as needed. The general categories most useful to me in estate planning files are the following:

1. **Communications:** As explained earlier, all records of communications with the client or others should be grouped together, regardless of whether it is a letter or notes of a meeting.

2. **Billing:** This includes everything relating to billing, including the client's fee agreement. If I had any guts, I would put this as number 1 and make communications number 2 because the fee agreement is the beginning of the lawyer-client relationship and essential to the file. I am not yet ready, however, to break with the prevailing legal "wisdom" that the correspondence folder should always be the first folder in the file.

3. **Client data:** This would include copies of questionnaires completed by the client, records of personal information, and your records of the client's asset information. This category should be broken into separate subfolders if there is a significant amount of information on separate assets or classes of assets or records of changes in those assets, such as life insurance illustrations or beneficiary designations, retirement plan information, or closely held business interests.

4. **Documents:** For simple estate plans, it may be sufficient to have one folder for the will and any other documents created. Other clients may require subfolders for wills, revocable trusts, irrevocable trusts, powers of attorney, and the like.

5. **Research:** The communications folder is intended to include records of communications with people outside of the firm. The research folder should hold notes and results of legal research, calculations, internal memoranda, and other lawyer notes or communications within the firm.

6. **Drafts:** By "drafts," I mean drafts of documents sent to the client for review. I find it convenient to keep these separate from other client communications only because drafts can be so bulky and can otherwise clutter up the correspondence folder. It is useful to keep drafts sent to the client for review because they are a record of the recommendations made to the client and the changes (if any) made at the client's request. Internal drafts of documents, never seen by the client or anyone outside of the firm, are generally worthless (except for internal finger-pointing if a mistake is made). They can be discarded soon after the documents are completed.

7. **Superseded documents:** This includes file copies of wills, revocable trusts, or other documents that are no longer in force. Some lawyers aren't sure that you should keep copies of superseded documents on the grounds that seeing what the will used to say might provide ammunition in a will contest or other dispute with or among the family. On the other hand, a series of consistent wills might be helpful in showing the testator's consistent intentions.

Estate or Trust Administration Files

General groupings of folders, with subfolders as needed, will also work for estate or trust administration files, but the general categories will be different.

1. **Communications:** All records of communications should be grouped together, regardless of whether it is a letter or notes of a meeting. In the case of an estate administration, it may be helpful to keep client communications and beneficiary communications in separate subfolders.

2. **Billing:** The fee agreement, bills, and records of costs advanced should be kept in a separate folder.

3. **Probate:** This folder or series of folders should contain the petition for probate, letters testamentary, and related pleadings or proceedings.

4. **Assets:** This would mainly cover assets owned at death but could include records of estate or trust investments purchased after death. This category should almost always be broken into separate subfolders for individual assets or classes of assets, so that information on particular assets (appraisals of real estate, Forms 712 for life insurance, etc.) can be located quickly and easily. Many estates lawyers like to organize their estate administration files in the same way as a federal estate tax return, so that all real estate information will be grouped under A or Schedule A, stocks and bonds under B or Schedule B, and so forth.

5. **Debts:** Records of debts owed at death can be kept separate, or they can be grouped with asset information, above. If you follow the organization of the federal estate tax return, then debts would be grouped under Schedule K, following the asset information found in Schedules A through I. (Schedule J would be administration expenses.)

6. **Receipts and disbursements:** These folders should include records of income receipts and disbursements and estate banking records.

7. **Tax returns:** The most significant tax return is usually the federal estate tax return (for those estates required to file one). Other tax returns include state death-tax returns, and there may be more than one if the decedent owned property in more than one state; the final lifetime income tax returns; and fiduciary income tax returns. Because of the size of the federal estate tax return, most lawyers will keep it separate from the folders for other types of tax returns and create subfolders for the backup documentation for the schedules and exhibits to the return.

8. **Research:** Similar to the research folder for estate planning files, this should hold the results of legal research, calculations, internal memoranda, and other lawyer notes or communications within the firm on issues relating to probate proceedings, tax returns, or other estate administration matters.

9. **Distributions:** It is possible to group the receipts, releases, family settlement agreement, and other records of the estate distribution with the probate proceedings. There is something aesthetically pleasing, though, in making the final distribution of the estate the last folder in the file.

File Retention and Destruction

It is probably part of the nature of lawyers to want to keep papers forever. We learn the value of documentary evidence and then hesitate to discard any piece of paper, no matter how trivial, out of fear that it might be a critical piece of evidence in some future lawsuit. We are taught the importance of careful drafting and accurate documentation of transactions and then can't stand the idea of destroying the beautiful documents that we have created.

Unfortunately (or fortunately, depending on your point of view), there is not enough space in the world to store all the documents created or collected by lawyers (or, even if there were enough space, you wouldn't want to pay to rent it). Sooner or later the time must come to dispose of unneeded files. Rather than agonize over every file or destroy files willy-nilly, it is better to have a plan for the orderly destruction of files whose time has come.

Closing the File

The best time to think about when to destroy the file is when it is being closed, immediately after all client work is finished. At that point, the file and its contents are fresh in your mind, and you can make an intelligent decision about the value of the file and when it will no longer be needed.

One suggestion: Never leave an important document in a closed file. A closed file should contain only correspondence, copies of documents, and your own records (notes, memoranda, time and billing records, etc.). Original contracts, wills, trusts, or other significant documents should be sent to the client or stored separately. They should *never* be kept in a closed file because it should always be possible to destroy a closed file without worrying about the contents. Therefore, one of the last steps in closing a file is to clean the file by returning all original documents to the client.

When to Destroy a File

As a general rule, you don't want to destroy a file as long as the contents might be relevant to a possible future dispute over actions recorded in the file. The dispute could be a malpractice action between you and the client (or the beneficiaries of the client after the client's death), a tax dispute involving tax returns filed or transactions recorded in the file, a dispute between the client and other persons (such as a dispute over a gift or a contract like a shareholder agreement), or a dispute among beneficiaries or other third parties. So, one measure of how long to keep a file would depend on the statutes of limitations for actions on the file.

Following are suggestions for timetables for the destruction of closed files of different types.

Current Clients

Generally speaking, the files of current clients should never be destroyed. It is too likely that questions will arise about the estate plan during the client's lifetime or after the client's death.

Unfortunately, the statute of limitations for legal malpractice usually does not begin to run until a harm has occurred. For estate planning lawyers, the statute of limitations for a faulty will or estate plan may not even begin to run until the client has died and the damage caused by the error or omission has occurred, though it may be years after the will or estate plan was created. In this respect, lawyers are like architects or engineers who may be sued for professional negligence after the negligence causes an injury many years after the negligence occurred.

For this reason, a "current" client is any living client who has in force documents that you created, since your professional advice can be questioned as long as those documents are in force. The fact that you have been terminated by a client and the client has sought other counsel does not necessarily mean that the client has revoked any of the wills or trusts that you created. Thus, you should not discard the client's file until you have been notified that the client has sought other counsel *and* that the documents that you created are no longer in force.

Past Clients

If a client has died and you are involved with the administration of the estate, consider the estate planning file to be on the same level with the estate administration file and destroy both files together. If a client has died and you are not involved with the estate administration, the file can probably be discarded after the statute of limitations has run on any possible claims by the estate or the estate beneficiaries.

Estate Administrations

An estate administration file should probably not be discarded at least until the statutes of limitations have run on all of the tax returns filed by or for the estate. This would be at least three years for most federal returns. Note that the statute of limitations for a federal return can actually be six years if there is a "substantial omission" from the return.

Estate Litigation

Assuming that there is a final judgment or final settlement of litigation, the problem is not the litigation itself. The problem is whether your client might decide that there was something wrong with the way that you handled the case. For that reason, the file should probably not be discarded until the statute of limitations has run on any possible professional claims.

Electronic Document Management

Managing your word processing documents is a little like managing your paper files. You want to find what you need when you need it, and you need a way of discarding what you don't need once you no longer need it.

Document management software can help organize the word processing files on your computer by identifying documents by the client name, the lawyer who created the document, the type or purpose of the document, the date the document was created or last modified, and other criteria. This can make it much simpler to find the documents that you need when you need them. Many document management programs also provide a way of archiving electronic documents (i.e., saving them to a separate disk or tape).

Computer hard disks keep getting bigger, so rather than taking the time to manage electronic files, there is a tendency to buy a new computer when the hard disk fills up. There are, however, advantages to learning to copy and archive client records from your hard disk to inexpensive diskettes or tapes.

◆ Unlike paper files, electronic files take up very little space, so you can maintain the electronic versions of the documents you created for as long as you want, and at almost no cost. For example, I recently transferred my archived client records (compressed to save disk space), including an electronic copy of almost every will and trust that I have created over the past twelve years, from a set of thirty 3.5-inch floppy diskettes to one Iomega Zip disk (which holds about 100 megabytes of information). New, inexpensive CD-R (compact disk-recordable) drives can record 360 megabytes of information on an optical disk that costs about two dollars.

◆ There is often a great deal of efficiency in being able to retrieve electronic copies of old wills and trusts. For example, a client may come back after several years and want to make changes to a will or other document that become quite simple if you can restore the earlier document, make the requested changes, and reprint the document instead of creating a new document from scratch. Even creating new documents for different clients can be easier if special or unusual provisions can be cut and pasted from older documents into new documents.

Estates lawyers should find document management software that will allow them to save and retrieve word processing documents more quickly and easily and to archive and index the word processing documents for closed client files. An estate planning or estate administration file may also generate many other types of computerized records, including electronic spreadsheets, electronic files for computerized tax returns, and computerized files for fiduciary accountings. If possible, these files should all be archived together, as part of the same client file, so that a client file can be re-created from a single source if necessary—and to avoid rummaging through the multiple archives of multiple software programs.

Getting the Work Done 7

"Would you tell me, please, which way I ought to walk from here?"

"That depends a good deal on where you want to get to," said the Cat.

"I don't care much where—" said Alice.

"Then it doesn't matter which way you walk," said the Cat.

"—so long as I get *somewhere*," added Alice as an explanation.

"Oh, you're sure to do that," said the Cat, "if you only walk long enough."

> —From Lewis Carroll's
> *Alice's Adventures in Wonderland*

THIS CHAPTER DISCUSSES how you can actually do the work for which you expect clients to pay you. As you might anticipate from the chapter's introductory quotation, the first step in deciding how to get the work done is to determine exactly what work needs to be done.

Most of this chapter focuses on how to use computer software and automation. There is, for example, a section on fiduciary accountings that discusses using accounting software, but there is no discussion of preparing accountings by hand. This is not an accident or an oversight.

Automation is the way to get things done, and using automation efficiently requires some planning and thought. As explained in the preface, however, it is not this book's purpose to duplicate the information in *Wills, Trusts, and Technology: An Estate Lawyer's Guide to Automation,* so many of the explanations of automation are necessarily general and do not include the detailed guidance related in that book.

Another point about this chapter is its emphasis on procedures. If you prefer to fly by the seat of your pants, ignoring checklists and guidelines, you're not going to like this chapter. Read it anyway.

Lastly, while this chapter addresses what needs to be done and possible ways to get it done, it doesn't discuss who should do it. Questions of delegation and allocation of work among employees are addressed in Chapter 8.

Where Are You Going?

In *Alice in Wonderland,* the Cheshire Cat points out to Alice that if you don't care where you are going, you can walk in any direction you want. Similarly, if you and your client don't have a clear idea of where you are going, it doesn't make much difference what steps you take to get there.

By "where you are going," I mean a precise idea of where you intend to end up, how long it will take you, and how much it will cost you. Before you start to work, make sure that you know what you are trying to accomplish.

Or, as carpenters say, measure twice and cut once.

Estate Planning

In estate planning, you want to have a clear idea of where the client is going to be once the estate plan is in place. This includes questions like these:

- ◆ What assets will be owned by the client, the client's spouse, the client's children (or grandchildren), in joint names of one or more of them, or in trusts for their benefit?

- ◆ What wills, revocable trusts, and powers of attorney will be in force to control the client's assets in the event of disability or death?
- ◆ What beneficiary designations will be in force for life insurance, retirement benefits, individual retirement accounts, and other plans or benefits within the client's control?

If you can't answer these questions, you can't know what is going to happen at the client's death. If you don't know what is going to happen at the client's death, you haven't really planned the estate.

Once you know where you are going, you can list the steps needed to get there. What documents must be created or amended? What assets need to be transferred? What beneficiary designations need to be changed? What forms are needed for those steps? Who will be responsible for each step?

A plan does not always have to be complete or final in every respect. Sometimes there are unanswered questions about certain gifts or certain assets, in which case you should plan to go as far as you can with what you know, letting the unanswered questions wait until you can answer them. For example, a client may be fairly certain about everything except whether to give the children voting or nonvoting stock in the family business. In that case, you can proceed with the wills, trusts, and other documents and steps while the client makes up his or her mind about the stock. When everything else is complete, the client may be in a better frame of mind to consider the situation and make a final decision.

The primary advantage of thinking things through and planning all the steps in advance is that you are more likely to anticipate and uncover problems. If, for example, you are talking about transferring real estate for gift or other reasons and you only talk about it in general terms, the client might not realize that filing fees and transfer taxes are required. If you go through the proposed transaction with the client in more detail, including all steps required to transfer the property and all filing fees and transfer taxes required, the client can make a more informed decision. You don't want to prepare all the deeds and documents and send them to the client only to have the client change his or her mind because of a fee or tax that you didn't discuss in advance.

Another advantage of thinking things through and planning the steps in advance is that you will know when you are finished. Then you can send the client a final bill.

Estate and Trust Administrations

In an estate administration, you should decide how the estate will be administered—and how and when it will be distributed—before the will is even probated. A good lawyer will meet with the family, get an estimate of the estate's size and nature, do a rough calculation of the death taxes payable, determine which assets will have to be sold to pay those taxes, and do a preliminary schedule showing the estate's distribution based on the terms of the will and the remaining assets. Ideally, this will all happen at the first meeting with the family, or soon thereafter. A complete plan and timetable for the administration of the estate would then be in place, from the probate of the will to the final distribution.

By making as many major decisions as possible in advance, with consideration for the entire estate, you avoid the risk of making poor decisions at the last minute, just before a critical deadline (or, worse, of missing a deadline entirely). The most time-consuming and expensive estates to administer are those that seem to lurch from filing deadline to filing deadline, with hurried decisions at each stage and no clear objectives. In addition, with no timetable for distribution and completion, estates often drag on longer than they should, resulting in unnecessary time expenditures that may not be covered by the fee agreement or that the client may be reluctant to pay.

Thinking about the ultimate distribution of the estate and the steps needed to get there can help you anticipate problems. In considering your goal, you may begin to think about the tax decisions or elections that must be made, the mechanics of selling or transferring assets, cash flow problems, third parties that must approve or be notified of asset transfers or other steps, and other possible complications. You might not realize these problems if you keep thinking only one step at a time.

As discussed in Chapter 5, another major benefit of setting definite objectives for an estate administration is that it gives the client realistic expectations and increases the likelihood that the client will be satisfied with the final result. Clients cannot see all of the problems and costs that can arise or all of the steps necessary to complete the estate administration. If you do not give the client a road map of what you expect to happen, each obstacle will increase the client's anger or frustration. However, if you can accurately chart most of the possible problems, the client may better appreciate your ability to avoid obstacles and surmount those that do arise.

Other Suggestions

Here are other suggestions that may be helpful in both estate planning and estate administration.

Use Checklists and Data Forms

Using a written form or checklist helps to ensure that you ask all the right questions, consider all the right issues, and take all the right steps in the right order and at the right time. Possible forms and checklists include the following:

- ◆ **Estate planning information:** Getting complete and accurate personal and asset information is essential for estate planning, and sending a new client a questionnaire is a good way to get the client to collect the necessary information before the initial meeting. Using a similar form during a client interview is also a good way of making sure that you don't forget to ask critical questions. The question I usually forget to ask is whether both husband and wife are U.S. citizens, which is too important to the federal estate tax marital deduction not to ask every client. (See Appendix D for a sample of an estate planning questionnaire.)

- ◆ **Probate information:** It's embarrassing to have to go back to a client right before the probate of the will or filing of the federal estate tax return to ask a question that you should have asked before. Once again, I have a favorite, which is that I can never remember to ask what year the decedent established his or her domicile. It is much better to have a form or checklist to give the executor or to use at the planning meeting with the executor. (See Appendix F for a sample form requesting or recording information about a decedent.)

- ◆ **Estate asset, receipt, and disbursement information:** If the executor will be keeping the estate checkbook and doing the legwork to collect asset information for the death tax returns (a procedure that seems increasingly common as clients try to reduce legal fees by doing more clerical work themselves), it is essential to give the executor clear written instructions of what records are needed. Otherwise, you will never get the requisite information to prepare complete and accurate returns. (See Appendix G for a sample checklist that can be used to collect financial information for probate and tax returns.)
- ◆ **Timetable of estate administration steps:** During the initial meeting with the decedent's family, you will want to review the steps necessary to complete the administration. Having a regular written checklist ensures that your timetable will be complete. Family members may also want a copy for their own information. (See Appendix H for a sample schedule.)

Use Tax or Other Forms as Reminders

Even if you are using a comprehensive checklist, there may be questions and issues that you have overlooked or that have not made their way into your checklist. One way to guard against this is to use blank tax returns as a check or reminder. Early in the administration, go through a blank tax form and read each question to make sure that you have not overlooked some potential problem or opportunity. Similarly, you can use a petition for probate as a reminder of the information you will need to probate the will.

If you haven't yet developed your own forms and checklists, consulting a tax return or other official form is a good way to start building your own.

Do Not Assume

Don't assume that you know the answer to a question that you haven't asked. Don't assume that your client knows to do something that you haven't told him or her about.

In estate planning, some of the most common problems are caused by bad assumptions about the value or title to assets. I once spent an entire hour with a client talking about a testamentary trust for her only daughter because the client had serious concerns about her daughter's ability to handle money. After we had settled on trustees, terms of the trust, and other provisions for her will, I finally thought to ask how her assets were currently titled. Of course, all of her assets were held jointly with her daughter, as joint tenants with right of survivorship.

In estate administrations, make sure that you ask about *all* the children or other heirs and whether a divorce from a "former" spouse was really final. If you don't ask, you don't know. Even if you do ask, you might not get the right answer, but then it's the client's problem, not yours. The client has every right to complain about a bad result that arises from your forgetting to ask a key question, but little right to complain when you asked the key question and the client gave you bad information.

Bill Frequently

Each bill sent to a client is, in effect, a statement of what has been done for the client. Thus, each bill is an opportunity to inform or remind the client of what has been done. This is valuable if there has been little other correspondence with the client. A client who receives a monthly summary of what has been done will be happier than one who hears nothing for months and then receives a lengthy and confusing statement of services rendered.

Many lawyers find it easier to bill when a major phase of a matter is completed or a major obstacle overcome. Forcing yourself to bill regularly can have the fringe benefit of encouraging you to complete at least some of the steps for your clients periodically to give yourself an excuse to send a bill. In fact, you might find it beneficial to agree with the client to break a particular representation into discrete phases and to send a bill at the end of each phase, rather than monthly or upon completion.

The Complete Representation

Having a complete plan for each matter you undertake for a client, with a clear understanding of where you are going and how you will get there, is good lawyering. Planning ahead should help to anticipate and avoid problems, develop better and more realistic client expectations, and increase client satisfaction.

Setting a specific goal for the outcome of a representation, creating and using checklists, reminding the client of steps that still need to be completed in each letter to the client, and billing regularly will all help to develop and carry out complete and satisfactory representations in estate planning and administrations.

Performing Tax Planning

Tax planning is a major part of most estate planning, including both lifetime estate planning and the postmortem tax planning that can be carried out even after the client has died.

Development of Recommendations

One of the first steps in tax planning is to identify those tax decisions or options that may be useful to the client. In compiling a list of possible recommendations, consider the following suggestions:

- ◆ Remember the client's goals. If all clients wanted to save all possible taxes at any cost, life would be fairly simple. However, clients usually have more than one goal, and some goals result in conflicts. For example, lifetime giving can save death taxes, but it can also diminish the client's financial security. You should look for recommendations that serve all of the client's goals, or at least as many of the important ones as possible.
- ◆ Bear in mind the client's personality and philosophy. Often the client's personality or life philosophy will enter into planning recommendations. For example, some clients like to keep things as simple as possible, while others seem to enjoy making their lives (and their children's lives) complicated. Some clients are quite concerned about keeping control of assets both during their lifetimes and afterward, while others are perfectly willing to entrust decisions to the fiduciaries they select.
- ◆ Narrow your focus to the issues most beneficial to the client. In other words, keep it simple. Some clients can consider thirteen different recommendations and approve all

of them. Most clients, though, have limited time and mental energy to spend on complicated legal matters. Make sure that you get the most important issues addressed before you confuse the client with other recommendations.

If a question arises about whether a possible recommendation will actually work for the client, either because of uncertainty in the tax laws or uncertainty about the financial results, it is a good practice to obtain preliminary approval from the client before spending time and money on legal research or tax projections. Otherwise, you might try to determine the feasibility or benefit of a tax technique of no interest to the client, owing to personal considerations or other factors of which you are unaware. The client will not want to pay for a recommendation that is of no use, and you will not want to spend uncompensated time doing what turns out to be an academic exercise. Talk to the client if you need to spend time on a recommendation and aren't sure if it will appeal to the client.

Presentation of Recommendations

Once you have decided on a set of recommendations for a client, you will need to present them and get the client's approval for the steps to be taken. You can do that orally, but there are good reasons to put at least some of the key recommendations in writing.

First, the client may need something in writing to remind him or her of what was recommended and why, or the client may want something to read and reread several times to understand the recommendations from the start of the process. Second, you may need something in writing to remind you of what was recommended and why. Lastly, you may need something in writing to protect yourself if the estate beneficiaries (or the client) later disagree with what was done and claim that the consequences were not adequately explained.

Explanations

Your explanations need to be in plain English. Whether they're written or oral, the best explanations of recommendations focus on the *why* and the *what*.

The why is the explanation of the benefit or goal that the rec-ommendation is intended to achieve. There should be at least one statement of the why that is as clear and simple as possible, even if other statements are added to provide details. For example, an explanation of a credit-bypass trust could include a statement like, "The family trust will save taxes for your children by keeping some property out of the survivor's estate." You can also describe the unified credit and how it works, but make sure that you don't detract from the essential message.

The what is the recommendation's meaning in nontax terms. Once again, there should be at least one clear and simple state-ment highlighting the recommendation's practical consequences. Returning to the example of the credit-bypass trust, a good expla-nation could include a statement like, "The assets of the family trust will be kept separate after the first death, and the survivor will get benefits from those assets if needed but will not be the owner of the assets." You can also include a more detailed expla-nation of the trustee's role and the disposition of the assets at the second death, but make sure that the issues of trust benefit and control remain clear.

Most tax planning recommendations are repeated for differ-ent clients, so it should be possible to establish fairly standard written explanations of recurring recommendations. You can then customize them for clients in letters or memos. Another alterna-tive is to create fairly comprehensive explanations of standard estate planning principles and recommendations and print them as a booklet or pamphlet. A brief cover letter to the client can high-light the important elements of the recommendations or those of most interest to the particular client. In either case, it may be pos-sible to automate the creation of customized client explanations in the same way that you can automate the drafting of wills and trusts, as described in a later section.

Illustrations

Every estate plan and tax recommendation should include a numer-ical illustration or projection of the tax consequences. You have to crank the numbers and show them to the client. There are several reasons why this is desirable, if not essential:

1. To make sure that the client understands the recommendation. For many clients, abstract explanations of theory
   will never sink in, and it is not until the clients have seen
   the numbers and worked through the calculations themselves, step by step, that they will understand what you
   are saying.
2. To make sure that you understand the recommendation.
   You can't really be sure that you are making the right recommendation until you run the numbers.
3. To protect yourself from unhappy beneficiaries. If a client
   fails to act on your recommendations or acts on your recommendations to the detriment of one or more beneficiaries, it will be much easier to defend your position and to
   establish that the client intended the complained-of
   results if you can show that the client saw the numbers
   and approved them.

Fortunately, various software packages can do estate tax and
other types of projections quickly and easily. Certain types of
estate planning recommendations, such as split-interest gifts that
require actuarial calculations, are practically impossible without
software that can do the necessary calculations. If you buy the
software that can do the calculations you want, you can produce
the illustrations by filling in the numbers and following the instructions that come with the software.

In the absence of specialized software, or for unusual calculations, it is possible to calculate and illustrate tax recommendations using general-purpose spreadsheet software. Most lawyers
and paralegals can learn how to use spreadsheets with only a few
hours of practice. Creating a customized illustration can often be
done in twenty or thirty minutes.

In selecting what software to buy, choosing what reports to
print from your software, or deciding how to set up a spreadsheet,
it is important to focus on the exact calculations and issues most
relevant to the client. Pages and pages of numbers may be worse
than no numbers at all, since the volume and complexity of the calculations may be too much for the client to sort through and com-
prehend. Ideally, a tax projection will show two columns, one

without the recommendation and one with the recommendation, and it will show the essential differences between the two results as simply and clearly as possible. That way, the client can compare them side by side with no extraneous details. (For an example, see Figure 1 on page 94.)

Regardless of whether you use commercial software or your own spreadsheet, be certain that all calculations are reviewed before being sent to the client. I do not mean that the lawyer must verify every number but that the results of the calculations are examined with an eye toward whether they make sense. Do the numbers seem to add up? Is the result what you would expect? If not, why not?

Visual Aids

Among the visual aids that can increase the client's understanding of the recommendations, a flowchart showing how assets are aggregated or divided upon death is helpful in estate planning. Boxes can represent different assets or groups of assets, as well as trusts, beneficiaries, or other distributees. Lines between the boxes can show how the estate or assets are divided or distributed. Different software products are available that will perform estate tax calculations and display the results in flowchart form. (See, for example, Figure 4 on page 96.) Some practitioners also prepare customized diagrams for clients with flowcharting software normally used to prepare diagrams of engineering processes or organizational charts. Some practitioners simply use a pencil and paper or different colored markers on a whiteboard to diagram the estate plan during client meetings. One recent technological development is electronic whiteboards, which can translate the writing on a whiteboard into electronic form and use a computer and printer to print a permanent copy of those diagrams. Regardless of how the diagrams are created, they have value to the client and to the client's understanding of the estate plan.

Another type of chart that may have value to the client is a bar graph, line graph, or pie chart for illustrating tax or financial projections. Although tables of numbers may provide an accurate illustration of a particular tax technique, many clients have difficulty comparing numbers. A graph that translates the numbers into lines or bars of different lengths may help the client grasp the impact of the numbers visually. Some possible uses of graphs or charts include the following:

♦ A pie chart showing how the estate is divided between the death tax liabilities and the beneficiaries before and after a particular estate planning recommendation (e.g., using a unified credit trust at the first death to decrease taxes at the second death). See, for example, Figure 3 on page 95.

♦ A line graph showing the increasing value of the assets owned by the children or other beneficiaries each year and the decreasing death tax liabilities each year as a result of an annual gift program. See, for example, Figure 2 on page 95.

♦ A bar chart showing the death tax liabilities, or amounts passing to the beneficiaries after taxes, with and without an irrevocable life insurance trust.

Drafting Documents

As part of the estate planning process, lawyers usually have to draft wills, trusts, and other kinds of documents to carry out the client's estate plan. In the past, most lawyers have had forms that they would mark up and give to a secretary to type. Word processing makes it possible for secretaries to start with an electronic form that does not have to be retyped, but effective use of computers means that the computer itself should assist in the creation of the document drafts.

Why Automate?

The economics of law practice make it increasingly less profitable for lawyers to spend much time drafting documents, particularly documents that contain standardized language, like wills and trusts. At the same time, increasingly sophisticated and consumer-conscious clients are dissatisfied with documents that they don't understand or that contain provisions that aren't relevant to them.

Faced with these conflicts, many lawyers are using computers to automate the will and trust drafting process. Why?

- ◆ To save time. An automated drafting system will allow you to create documents in less time. Many lawyers who have automated their document drafting report that they can produce wills, trusts, and other estate planning documents in a third to a fourth of the time needed without automation.
- ◆ To reduce errors. An automated document drafting system should reduce errors and increase the quality of your work product. Names spelled correctly at the beginning of the document are spelled correctly throughout. The automation process is usually able to ensure consistency within documents and avoid possible legal errors, so that a surviving spouse as sole trustee is not given unregulated discretion to distribute income or principal from the unified credit trust in which the spouse is also a beneficiary (because those powers could cause unnecessary estate tax at the spouse's death).
- ◆ To increase customization. An automated drafting system should also permit greater customization of documents to suit the individual client's needs. Unnecessary provisions can be eliminated more easily. Thus, a client with only individuals as executors and trustees does not need to read provisions regarding the compensation of corporate fiduciaries, and a retired client with only certificates of deposit does not need to read lengthy provisions regarding the administration of closely held businesses.

Automation Methods

There are at least three different ways to implement an automated drafting system:

1. **Word processing:** Many lawyers find that they can create an acceptable system that prepares documents by filling in names and other information using only their word processing software's merge and macro features. Selecting alternate clauses is usually too difficult without getting into some fairly complicated programming. This kind of

system usually requires that each type of will and trust be reduced to a different form. The user can then select the desired form and enter the information needed to complete it, with the names and other information already filled in.

2. **Document drafting engines:** Special software programs can insert names and other information into forms as well as select alternate clauses or phrases to put into documents. Simple document drafting engines are often included with case management software so that lawyers can draft letters and other documents using client data already in the case management system. These programs allow law firms to create drafting systems that are easier to modify, or more powerful, than using only a word processing program.

3. **Automated forms systems:** A third choice is to buy forms that have already been automated by someone else. Several systems have been developed for drafting wills and trusts, and it is easier for a firm to buy and use those kinds of systems than for the firm to automate its own forms. The firm that buys an automated forms system, though, is pretty much stuck with the style and content of the forms. Although many systems allow users to change the text of individual clauses, making widespread changes can be difficult and time-consuming.

Which approach a firm should take depends on (1) whether it has the technological and management skills, as well as the desire, to automate its own forms; and (2) the firm's substantive legal judgments about the suitability of the automated forms systems that are available commercially.

Drafting Tips

Here are some practical (nonautomation) tips for efficiently drafting documents that should build client satisfaction.

- ◆ Put the important elements first. Don't make the client wade through pages of definitions and boilerplate to get to the provisions that the client really needs to read, understand, and approve. For example, the appointment of executors and trustees is important to the client and so should be at the beginning of wills and trusts, not at the end or in the middle. Similarly, directions regarding payment of debts and taxes really aren't interesting and should be moved back into the boilerplate (assuming it is even necessary to have a direction to pay debts). Assume that your client has a limited amount of time for you (or perhaps a limited attention span), and arrange your documents accordingly.

◆ Try to eliminate pronouns and gender-sensitive words. For example, when referring to the income for the client's child, don't refer to "his or her benefit" but rather "the child's benefit." This simplifies drafting and allows documents to be adapted to other clients more quickly. Don't refer to the client's husband or wife as a "spouse," but do refer to "my husband's maintenance and support" and not "his maintenance and support." That way, you can use a simple search and replace to convert quickly from "husband" to "wife" as necessary when adapting the document.

◆ Write revocable trusts in the first person (e.g., "I hereby establish a trust") rather than the third person (e.g., "The grantor hereby establishes a trust"). That makes it easier to copy will provisions into trusts and vice versa. For similar reasons, organize the clauses of your revocable trusts in the same order as your wills, to the extent possible. Then you need to remember only one document structure, instead of two, and you can find relevant clauses more quickly when reviewing or modifying drafts.

◆ Limit the number of drafts you go through before you send the documents to the client. It's common to read the first (or second) draft and realize that some language could be improved. However, if you are reading the third draft and still changing words around, the odds are excellent that you're not really improving the document, just making a different mistake. If you think that what you have drafted might not be exactly what the client wants, but you are not sure, go ahead and send the draft to the client, explain your uncertainty, and ask the client what to do. That's better than wasting more time changing the document to something the client might not like either.

◆ Keep it as simple and as clear as possible. Clients like to understand what they are signing. They won't be happy if they have to struggle to understand what you have written. Make the structure of the document (and your recommendations) as simple as possible. For example, don't write two testamentary trusts for two beneficiaries if the terms of the trusts are essentially the same and could be stated once for both beneficiaries. Don't try to consolidate language, though, if there are so many differences and exceptions between the two trusts that the result is confusing. Write in simple, declarative sentences in the active voice, with the fewest words possible. If you are not sure how to write clearly, take the time to read (or reread) *The Elements of Style* by Strunk and White (Macmillan Publishing).

Preparing Fiduciary Accountings

There are two ways to prepare a fiduciary account: the right way and the usual way. The usual way is to keep accurate records of receipts and disbursements through income ledgers and checkbook registers. When it is time to prepare a final (or required) accounting for the court or the beneficiaries, a paralegal goes through all the bank statements, brokerage statements, and other records and tries to put together an accounting that balances.

The right way to prepare a fiduciary accounting is to make it an integral part of your estate or trust administration. As soon as the opening inventory is established, the data should be entered into an accounting program so that the inventory can be printed and, if necessary, edited and updated. As debts or expenses are paid, assets are sold, or income is received, that information should also be entered into the accounting program. When brokerage and bank statements are received each month, the statements should be reconciled against the accounting program's balances and any errors corrected immediately so that a complete accounting that is accurate to within a month can be printed at any time.

Advantages of Keeping Accountings Current

The right way, which uses automation to prepare and update accountings every month, has a number of advantages over the usual way, which is to prepare an accounting only at the termination of the estate or trust.

- Trying to prepare a final accounting all at once can be tedious. By preparing the accounting in smaller monthly steps, there is less strain on the lawyers and paralegals and less boredom with what otherwise can seem to be an extremely repetitive task. Less boredom means a more enjoyable practice and, in most cases, fewer mistakes and greater efficiency.
- Preparing an accounting contemporaneously, in monthly steps, makes it easier to find and correct mistakes. Typically an accounting for a period of two or more years does not balance the first time, with perhaps three to six errors causing the imbalance. Finding each mistake may be difficult when you do not know when the mistake occurred. In addition, once a mistake is found, it could require an explanation (e.g., why was a $500 check sent to John Smith last August?) that may be difficult to reconstruct after a long period of time, either because memories have faded or because the associate or paralegal who was then involved with the estate or trust is no longer with the firm. By reconciling bank accounts and brokerage accounts monthly, it becomes easier to find and correct mistakes.
- Providing timely interim accountings can improve relationships with beneficiaries. Many beneficiaries become worried or suspicious if they never receive information or don't receive information for long periods of time. Quarterly accountings give the beneficiaries timely and accurate information that can help avoid unnecessary conflicts or misunderstandings. (Because fiduciary accounts usually are cash accountings, not accrual accountings, they usually do not show unpaid liabilities, which can make an estate with unpaid death taxes appear much larger than it really is. To avoid misunderstandings by beneficiaries, interim account-

ings should show any unpaid death taxes or projected expenses as unpaid liabilities that reduce the estate's value.)

♦ Contemporaneous accountings can be used as an internal audit procedure to protect the firm from dishonest or incompetent employees. Too many lawyers have entrusted paralegals and secretaries with depositing fiduciary receipts and then discovered funds were missing. By requiring that bank and brokerage statements be reconciled monthly and periodically comparing the fiduciary accountings with the statements, lawyers can help fulfill their fiduciary duty to safeguard client funds.

Management Issues

Unfortunately, many lawyers believe that fiduciary accountings are only needed if court approval is required and that accounting can be ignored if the beneficiaries are willing to waive a court accounting. Although fiduciary accounting software is most often used to prepare accountings to be filed in court, the software can provide benefits to the administration of almost every estate.

First there is the benefit of informed consents. Is an accounting really unnecessary if the beneficiaries are willing to waive a court accounting? In the absence of a complete accounting, a beneficiary might be able to challenge any waiver on the grounds that the oral or incomplete information that was given was misleading. A family agreement or informal settlement should be harder to challenge, and may also be easier to obtain, if there has been a complete and detailed accounting to the beneficiaries in the same form that would otherwise have been filed in court.

In addition, an accurate fiduciary accounting makes it much easier to prepare accurate death tax returns and income tax returns. In the absence of a complete and balanced account, it is possible to overlook assets, income, or deductions that would have been recorded if an accounting had been prepared. As a result, some lawyers will not prepare a tax return until an accounting has been prepared and shown to balance. A corollary of this policy is that the accounting should match the tax treatment of the various items, or accommodate the tax treatment of the items whenever possible. For example, separate taxable interest income from tax-free interest income so that the accounting shows a sub-total of the taxable interest that can be used in the fiduciary income tax returns.

A current accounting may also make it easier to manage the assets of the estate and respond to questions from clients and beneficiaries. What assets are on hand? What needs to be distributed or paid? How much cash is there? What could be sold if more cash is needed? All these questions can be easier to answer if all the asset and income information is in an accounting rather than scattered through multiple statements and records.

For all of the preceding reasons, you should establish procedures ensuring that all fiduciary accounts are kept current and reconciled monthly and that the responsible lawyer can review those accountings regularly.

Preparing Tax Returns

As previously noted, death-tax returns and fiduciary income tax returns are usually much easier to prepare (and more accurately prepared) once an accounting has been prepared for the estate or trust. It is therefore recommended that tax returns be based on the accounting for the estate or trust, with whatever additional information or changes to information may be needed to accommodate the differences between fiduciary accounting for an estate or trust and tax returns for the estate or trust.

In-House Preparation

Once the necessary information has been collected, tax returns can be prepared by a firm in one or more of the following ways.

◆ Software can be used to prepare estate, gift, and income tax returns, prompting for needed information and performing necessary calculations. Some software is also integrated with fiduciary accounting software, so inventory assets can be transferred directly to death-tax returns or receipts and disbursements can be transferred directly to income tax returns.

◆ On-line services can prepare tax forms based on the information supplied by the lawyer or paralegal. This approach can result in less cost per return once you take into account the cost of tax preparation software and the time needed to learn to use it effectively.

◆ CD-ROMs are also available that can fill in and print a large variety of returns, although computational abilities are usually limited (addition and subtraction only) or nonexistent. These kinds of CD-ROMs are still useful for filling in the forms (serving as a kind of "glass typewriter") and for providing a library of forms that are instantly accessible.

◆ It is still acceptable to fill in forms by hand. In fact, for relatively simple forms or forms that are not often needed, this approach may be more effective than learning how to automate tax return preparation.

It is not necessary to use the same procedure for every return. Return preparation software might be purchased for returns that are prepared regularly (e.g., federal estate tax returns) while some simpler returns are still prepared by hand (e.g., fiduciary income tax returns).

Outside Services

Another option is to contract out with an accountant, independent paralegal, or other third party for the preparation of the return. This may be a matter of client preference (such as a client who has an accountant who does all the client's tax returns); a matter of local custom (in some parts of the country, it is unusual for lawyers to prepare fiduciary income tax returns, although most lawyers throughout the United States will usually prepare the death tax returns for an estate); or a matter of perceived efficiency (the law firm may not have the volume of returns to justify hiring or training a paralegal or buying new software).

Asset Valuations

Estate and gift tax returns require valuations of assets, including publicly traded securities. There are several ways to obtain valuations of these kinds of securities:

1. Ask the broker holding the securities (or some other friendly broker) to look up the values for you. This is certainly an inexpensive approach, but the problem with this method is that brokers frequently do not understand that values for estate and gift tax purposes are based on the averages of high and low prices, not the closing price. (They also frequently fail to take into account accrued interest on bonds, and stocks sold ex dividend.)
2. Collect the business sections of your newspaper and keep them for a year or more so that you can look up the published market prices.
3. Look up on-line valuations on the Internet or through other on-line databases.
4. Contract with a service provider that performs valuations for a fixed fee for each security. Communications can be on-line or by fax or telephone. These services can usually value municipal bonds and other securities not listed in newspapers or general databases.

Valuation of real estate, privately held businesses, and other types of property without values listed on an open exchange usually requires the services of an appraiser.

Dealing with General Technology Problems

When trying to generate work product in a modern law office, lawyers and staff often run into stubborn little problems. There are, however, relatively simple solutions to some of them.

Completion of Forms

Computers and laser printers have replaced typewriters in most offices. How then do you fill in preprinted forms? Most courts still require that preprinted forms be completed in probate proceedings but won't accept forms filled in by hand. What do you do?

The simplest solution is to scan the form into a computer, use the computer to "type" onto the form, and then print out the scanned image of the form with the "typed" words superimposed on the printed image of the form. Most scanners sold today include scanning software that makes this quite easy to do. In fact, many programs will automatically figure out where the blanks are in the form and let you fill in the form like the computer was a "glass typewriter," using the tab key to go from blank to blank, much like the forms that come on CD-ROMs (see the earlier section on tax returns). It is also possible to save the form and use it over and over again for different clients. And the printed result is often indistinguishable from a high-quality photocopy.

Without a scanner, or for a form that can't be scanned for some reason, the choices are more awkward and time-consuming:

1. Figure out how to arrange the words on a blank page in the right spaces, then transfer the words to the form. WordPerfect includes an advance feature that can be used to position words on a page at a stated distance from the top and side of the page. If the words can be printed onto the right spots and the printed form can be run through the printer, the form can be filled in using the computer and printer.

2. "Fake" the form. Using your word processing software, you may be able to match the fonts and spacings on the form and print a duplicate that is identical to the official form in content and substantially similar in appearance. This should be acceptable if the court or agency allows the use of a substantially similar form. (Do *not* try to trick the court or agency into believing that you are using a copy of the official form.)

3. For forms like inventories, death-tax return schedules, and other forms that have only a few blanks but require a lot of data, it may be sufficient to type or write in "See Attached" and then attach a computer-generated list or word processing document with the necessary information. This might seem like a transparent evasion of the form, yet it works surprisingly often.

Letterhead

Printing on letterhead often creates technological problems. The first page must be on one kind of paper, while the second page must be on continuation stock. That means that sheets must be fed manually in the right order or, alternatively, that printers must be purchased with multiple paper bins and the software configured to pull the first page from one bin and the other pages from other bins, while other kinds of documents are printed from paper in a third bin.

A solution for many firms is to print letterhead using the word processing program itself, either using text and fonts within the software or a graphical image of the letterhead imbedded in the template for the letter. In that way, you need only two types of paper and two paper bins, one with stationery for letters (the software generating the headers for the first letterhead page and the following continuation pages) and another bin with plain paper for other documents.

Envelopes and Labels

It is often awkward to prepare envelopes and labels with a word processor, but the right supplies and setup can make the task ridiculously easy. Most word processing software now comes with envelope procedures built in. It is worth your firm's time to make sure that your word processing program can print a label just by selecting (i.e., highlighting) the address in a letter and then clicking on a preprogrammed button or selecting a special menu choice. Similar procedures can be set up to print mailing labels from selected text.

The problem with printing mailing labels is that laser-printer label stock usually has six labels to a sheet, and it becomes difficult to print only one label from a sheet that has already had a label printed from it. There are interesting solutions from legal suppliers. One solution is an envelope-size sheet with a mailing label where the envelope address normally goes. By telling the program to print an envelope but inserting the special label, you get a mailing label instead of an envelope. A solution that wastes less paper is a "two-up sheet," which has two mailing labels side-by-side on one sheet the size and shape of an envelope. You can print one label on the left half of the sheet, then rotate the sheet around and feed it backward to print on the other half, which was the right half and is now the left half. This setup makes it possible to use both labels even though the software printed each label in what it thought was the same position on the sheet.

Finding and Archiving Documents

After creating a large number of letters, wills, trusts, powers of attorney, accountings, court pleadings, and other kinds of electronic documents, many firms discover that they have increasing trouble finding the right documents among the mass of files that have accumulated on their computer system.

One solution is document management software. It allows documents to be classified by client, document type, version (or draft) number, and other criteria. It creates a database of that information so that the right document (and the right version of the document) can be found quickly and easily. The software should also be able to compress and save (or archive) to another disk any documents that are not currently active, while maintaining a database of where the documents have been stored. Using the database of archived files, you can find and restore an old file fairly easily, so that old wills, trusts, or other documents can be retrieved and reused for the same client or other clients with similar needs. For example, if a client comes back after three years wanting a relatively simple change in a will or revocable trust, it may be easier to retrieve the old word processing file, make the change, and reprint the document for execution than it would be to create a new document or a codicil or amendment.

See Chapter 6 for additional information on electronic document management.

Libraries and Research Materials

Most lawyers have to hit the books sooner or later. The question to ask here is, which books?

Basic Materials

Every practice needs some research materials for quick reference, even if the local law library or online sources are available for in-depth research. The following basic materials will be helpful in almost any estates practice:

- Federal estate tax materials, with the relevant portions of the Internal Revenue Code and regulations at a minimum. Relatively inexpensive CD-ROMs are available that include the complete Internal Revenue Code, regulations, IRS public and private rulings, tax court cases, and other materials, all of which can be searched for words, phrases, or section references.
- Relevant state and local statutes and rules, including the state probate code, any state death tax statutes and regulations, and local probate court rules.
- One or two texts that provide an overview of estate taxation, or specific guidance on tax techniques of special value to the firm's practice. Examples of a general reference might be *Modern Estate Planning* by Ernest D. Fiore, Mark L. Friedlich, Alan Chevat, and Thomas McInerney (published by Matthew Bender & Co.), *Federal Taxation of Income, Estates and Gifts,* by Boris I. Bittker and Lawrence Lokken (Warren, Gorham & Lamont), *Estate Planning Service* (a CD-ROM from Research Institute of America), and *Tax Planning for Family Wealth Planning* by Howard M. Zaritsky and Stephan R. Leimberg (Warren, Gorham & Lamont). A more specialized text might be something like *Tax Planning with Life Insurance* by Howard M. Zaritsky and Stephan R. Leimberg (Warren, Gorham & Lamont).
- A text or manual with forms and procedures specific to the particular state or county. For example, a standard text in Pennsylvania is *Pennsylvania Orphans' Court Practice* by Raymond M. Remick (The Beisel Company). At a more local level, the Philadelphia Bar Association has published two different books, *Practice and Procedure before the Register of Wills and the Orphans' Court Division in Philadelphia* and *Forms for Use Before the Register of Wills and the Orphans' Court Division in Philadelphia.*

The exact size and nature of each firm's library will depend on the firm's practice and needs as well as other resources available to it, such as local law libraries and other law firms' materials.

Print versus CD-ROM

Although some had predicted that CD-ROMs would replace printed books, the fact is that books still have their uses. Books do not require any power, and there are never any technical problems "installing" them. More importantly, books are easier to read than the little letters on a computer screen. The human eye can scan a page and jump to the relevant section head or topical sentences much faster than computers can refresh a screen. You can flip through several pages of a book and find what you're looking for much faster than you can scroll through a computerized text.

The advantage of a CD-ROM lies in the search capabilities, which is why CD-ROM tax libraries with statutes, regulations, cases, and rulings are so useful. More than just a book, and more than just text, a CD-ROM allows users to search for words, phrases, and section references and quickly display the relevant documents or portions of documents.

Although CD-ROMs can be more expensive than comparable print versions, the actual production costs are less. Once a master CD has been created, the cost of duplicating the disc is measured in pennies, not dollars. A master disc can be created using hardware and software that cost only a few hundred dollars. As a result, low-cost CD-ROMs have been driving down the costs of both printed books and on-line legal research services for many specialized practices.

Lastly, the cost of a CD-ROM must be compared to the cost of on-line research, through traditional services like Westlaw and LEXIS and new subscription services available through the Internet. For research materials that will be needed frequently, buying the CD-ROM version may be cost-effective. If, however, the firm's legal research only rarely requires certain state and federal resources, it may be more economical to subscribe to an on-line service on a per-transaction basis and be billed only for the statutes, cases, and other materials actually retrieved.

Both CD-ROM and the Internet have created a number of new choices and new dilemmas. When shopping for library resources, it is important to consider how the materials will be used, as well as how often, in choosing between print, CD-ROM, and on-line versions.

Periodicals

In addition to standard reference works, practitioners need legal periodical subscriptions to stay on top of the latest developments in federal estate tax planning and estate and trust law generally. Good sources of current information include *Estate Planning* from Warren, Gorham & Lamont, *Trusts and Estates* from Argus Communications, and *Probate & Property* from the ABA Section of Real Property, Probate, and Trust Law.

Internet Services

Internet access is increasingly important to lawyers. It is particularly important to solos and small firms because the Internet provides inexpensive news, research tools, and opportunities to communicate with other practitioners and to maintain professional contacts. A local Internet service provider (ISP) should be able to give you unlimited access at a reasonable cost, as well as disk space for your own Web pages. (Consider also getting your own domain name so that your e-mail address and Web site address can remain the same even if you change ISPs.)

Other Resources

A law firm with a limited budget (and aren't all budgets limited?) should become familiar with—and provide needed support to—any law libraries supported by the local bar associations or local courts. Law schools may also be able to provide access to more unusual materials. In addition, many law firms in close proximity will agree to share books through interfirm loans.

Personnel 8

> The greatest improvement in the productive
> powers of labour, and the greater part of the
> skill, dexterity, and judgment with which it is
> any where directed, or applied, seem to have
> been the effects of the division of labour.
>
> —Adam Smith,
> *The Wealth of Nations,* Book I, Chapter 1

To delegate, or not to delegate? That is the
question.

Many books, articles, and seminars will tell you
to "leverage" your time through effective use of staff.
By delegating work to paralegals and associates and
billing for their time in excess of their salaries, you
can make a profit from their time as well as your own.
In an estates practice, what kinds of tasks can be delegated and what kinds of tasks are better performed
by the managing lawyer?

The Employee Cost-Benefit Equation

Although the benefits of delegating are frequently
explained, the costs are often overlooked. The key
cost is the time spent in communication and supervi-

sion. The effective use of employees is based on the assumption that the employee can achieve the same result as the lawyer but at less cost owing to the employee's lower compensation. To figure the cost of using a subordinate employee, the supervising lawyer must take into account the time needed to instruct the employee in what needs to be done. For routine tasks, this will be a minor cost. For a secretary or paralegal who already knows how to prepare a petition for probate, preparing other types of probate pleadings will not be that difficult. Unless a paralegal has been trained in fiduciary accounting or has a background in basic accounting practices, however, training him or her to prepare fiduciary accountings can be time-consuming and represent a large investment of time—and therefore money.

Supervision also requires time. You can't just hand a job to a secretary or paralegal and assume that it will be done correctly. Letters, pleadings, and other forms of documents must all be reviewed, as well as tax returns and financial accountings. Supervision is not just a matter of quality control but can be a matter of economic survival. Stories periodically appear about law firms discovering that a bookkeeper or paralegal had been "borrowing" funds of an estate or trust, but usually only after several hundred thousand dollars were missing. Those sorts of losses can be avoided with a few minutes of reviewing the right records and accounts each month.

Another cost is client relations. To use an associate or paralegal efficiently, the employee should be able to talk to the client to get information and explain routine matters. If the partner or senior lawyer must be involved in every client communication, the senior lawyer actually becomes a messenger for the junior employee, running back and forth between the client and the junior employee with messages. If, on the other hand, the associate or paralegal is put into direct contact with the client, the client may feel put off or slighted by dealing with a lower-ranking employee. To use the associate or paralegal effectively, it is necessary to educate the client about the value of using other employees, and to reassure the client that the senior lawyer will be supervising the employees and will always be available to answer questions or deal with any problems that might arise.

Lastly, the economic benefit of paralegals in estate adminis-trations can vary from state to state. For example, New Jersey decisions have actually disallowed any compensation to a law firm for paralegal time spent in administering an estate, only lawyer time being compensable and paralegal costs being considered an overhead expense to be included in the lawyer's hourly rates. For-tunately, that attitude is usually a short-lived minority view, not the general rule, but it is still necessary to know what fees and costs can be recovered from an estate before assuming that para-legal time can be billed to the estate in the same way that a law-yer's time is billed.

Secretaries

What is a secretary? Just as inflation reduces the value of money over time, the passage of time often debases the value of words, so a word like *unique,* which means (or should mean) one of a kind, becomes a synonym for unusual. Similarly, the secretary's role is not as important as it formerly was.

The original meaning of secretary was a confidential adviser, usually to a king or government (hence, "secretary of state"). At sometime in the distant past, nobles, landed gentry, or others of wealth acquired a need for a "personal secretary" who would keep track of finances, business and personal correspondence, and other confidential matters. In the offices of lawyers and merchants, those who wrote out documents or other kinds of paperwork were clerks or copyists. Some successful merchants or lawyers eventually decided that they needed personal assistants, and they decided to call those personal assistants "secretaries," just like the secretaries employed by the nobility and the gentry. The introduction of the typewriter was probably the final blow to the original meaning of secretary because eventually every typist or stenographer was referred to as a secretary, even though he or she kept no secrets and gave no advice. So the role of a secretary went from being an adviser to the king to being a typist and file clerk in an office "cube farm."

But enough of this etymological chitchat. The point is that you shouldn't assume that you need someone to fill a particular meaning of a word. Instead, you should decide what tasks you need performed and what kind of person would be suited to fill those tasks. Do you need a typist, a filing clerk, an office manager, or someone else entirely?

Proper use of computers can drastically reduce the need for a typist or stenographer. Document assembly software can prepare first drafts of wills, trusts, powers of attorney, contracts, and form letters that are almost complete, requiring only some final revisions and customization before they are ready for the client. Usually it is more efficient for lawyers to learn basic word processing skills and review and complete the final drafts working at the computer rather than printing out the documents, marking them up, having a typist enter the changes into the computer, and then reviewing the changes to see if the typist made any mistakes. Even more remarkable is the advance in speech recognition technology, which now makes it possible for a lawyer to dictate to a computer and for the computer to type the words into the letter or contract.

Using computers to prepare documents and teaching lawyers basic word processing skills has drastically reduced the need for the secretary-typist. Many law firms and law departments have reduced their secretarial staffs from one to every one or two lawyers to one secretary for every four, five, or six lawyers.

Other tasks that secretaries may be called upon to perform include time entry, billing, and simple bookkeeping of receipts and disbursements. While those tasks can (and should) be delegated by lawyers to employees, many lawyers hire part-time employees or consultants rather than full-time secretaries.

The use of computers has made many aspects of time entry and billing directly accessible to lawyers. Just as many lawyers find it faster and more efficient to do their own text editing of documents, so many lawyers prefer to enter and edit their own time records. They may even review and edit final bills electronically, in which case the bookkeeping required of secretaries or other employees may be reduced to recording receipts and disbursements.

The one thing a computer still can't do is file the right papers in the right file folder or file jacket. I have never had a secretary who was good at those tasks either, though, and have resigned myself to spending my own time putting papers where I want to find them later.

The point is that it should no longer be assumed that every lawyer needs a secretary. Using computers, lawyers can efficiently and effectively handle many tasks traditionally performed by secretaries, including routine correspondence, document drafting, time entry, and even billing. Other tasks that should still be delegated, or that secretaries sometimes perform, such as bookkeeping, filing, and other kinds of clerical work, might be handled by paralegals or by part-time employees or consultants.

Paralegals

By paralegal, I mean any assistant who can apply some knowledge of law or rules of court to the performance of his or her duties. Many experienced legal secretaries have performed tasks that might now be classified as paralegal tasks, such as preparing court pleadings and drafting simple wills and trusts. For simplicity, I have assumed that secretarial tasks are limited to typing, filing, and other clerical tasks requiring no legal knowledge, while all tasks requiring some legal background should be grouped together and discussed as paralegal tasks.

The following paragraphs review the various types of work described in Chapter 7 and consider which might be appropriate (or inappropriate) for delegation to a paralegal.

Projections and Presentations

If the client is to be given a written summary of estate planning projections and recommendations, a paralegal could be very helpful in preparing that presentation.

During the first client meeting or through correspondence before the client meeting, all of the necessary asset and personal information will be collected from the client, if possible in a standardized form used by the law firm for this purpose. After reviewing this information, an experienced estates lawyer should be able to make a quick list of estate planning techniques or decisions that might be of interest to the client or should be considered by the client. This selection should be possible because most estate planning is based on a relatively small number of principles and tax techniques.

Once the lawyer has decided on a list of possible recommendations to present to the client, preparing the written presentation should involve combining three types of information:

1. Explanations of the recommendations
2. Numerical projections showing the results of the recommendations
3. Graphs or charts summarizing or illustrating the recommendations themselves or the calculations based on the recommendations.

The explanations should be relatively routine, not varying greatly from client to client, so that a first draft could be assembled from form language prepared for this purpose or adapted from similar presentations to other clients.

The numerical projections should also be mechanical, based on the client data already assembled and the possible recommendations selected by the lawyer. Like the explanations of the recommendations, the calculations should follow standard patterns. Using estate planning software or spreadsheet templates developed by the law firm for this purpose, a paralegal should be able to enter the appropriate client data and do the calculations and projections necessary to illustrate each recommendation.

A lawyer or law firm should also develop a standard collection of charts or graphs to illustrate particular estate plans or particular tax planning calculations. Once again, given the lawyer's list of recommendations to be presented, the client data, and guidance in the preparation of the appropriate charts or graphs for those recommendations, a paralegal should be able to complete appropriate illustrations for the client.

The preparation of written estate planning recommendations requires a lawyer for the initial selection of appropriate recommendations to the client and a final review to make sure that the calculations are correct and the written presentation is consistent with the estate plan that the lawyer envisioned. The mechanics of assembling the presentation, however, often requires a certain amount of clerical work, such as the organization and summation of client asset information and the assembly and appropriate modification of the text and illustrations for the presentation. Some legal training is still needed to put the right numbers in the right calculations and to be sure that the right calculations, text, and graphical illustrations go with the right recommendations.

Because the assembling of estate planning presentations requires some legal training but little discretion or legal judgment, and can be based on forms and guidelines prepared by a lawyer in advance, it is well suited to delegation to a paralegal.

Document Drafting

At first blush, drafting wills, trusts, and other estate planning documents might seem to be appropriate for a paralegal, just like the preparation of estate planning presentations. However, there are significant differences.

Drafting wills and trusts is often much more complex, requiring more customization and legal judgment, than the recommendations leading up to the wills and trusts. The recommendations themselves can be fairly general descriptions of tax principles that apply to many people in similar ways. The operative wills and trusts, though, often need to be customized to the client's particular situation. Usually a lawyer must exercise legal judgment in selecting the provisions that go into a will and trust, and in modifying standard provisions to meet any special needs of the client.

For example, a recommendation that a client's will include a unified credit or bypass trust to reduce estate tax can be explained in general terms that would apply to most people. The actual trust terms desired by the client can be fairly complex, involving questions of whether the surviving spouse and the children are income beneficiaries, or only some of them, the standards to apply in allocating income, the standards to apply in distributing principal, and whether the surviving spouse should have a limited power of withdrawal or a limited power of appointment. A number of legal questions may arise, such as whether the surviving spouse can serve as the sole trustee with only ascertainable standards or as a co-trustee-trustee, or whether the power to apply principal for the support of minor children should be excluded, and so forth.

If the firm uses a manual drafting system, in which documents are assembled by pulling together different clauses and phrases into a single document, using a paralegal might be appropriate

because of the time and effort needed to carry out the drafting decisions of the lawyer. Considerable time and effort may be necessary
to select, cut and paste, and put together the various clauses into a
first draft, ready for the lawyer's review and modification. If, however, the firm has an automated system that will assemble the documents automatically, based on information supplied to the
computer, the paralegal may be more of a hindrance than a help.
Because the system is automated and requires only the entry of the
drafting decisions, the computer will handle the mechanical assembly of the document that would have been performed by the paralegal in a manual system. In the time required to explain to the
paralegal what kinds of documents to draft, what provisions to put
into the documents, and how to answer the various questions
asked by the computer, the lawyer can instruct the computer
directly and receive back a first draft, ready for review and editing.

It has already been suggested that a computer's power to
draft documents may reduce the need for a secretary. For similar
reasons, the computer may make paralegals unnecessary to the
drafting process as well.

Probate Procedures

Many of the probate petitions, notices to beneficiaries, and other
pleadings and documents needed for the probate of a will and
related court proceedings are relatively routine. They can be prepared by paralegals from the information collected regarding the
decedent, the decedent's assets, the will, and the beneficiaries.

Fiduciary Bookkeeping and Accounting

The collection of estate or trust assets, both principal and income,
the payment of debts, the accounting for all of those transactions,
and the paperwork necessary for the distribution of an estate or
trust all entail clerical work better suited to paralegals than lawyers. The production of fiduciary accounts in a form suitable for
filing in court also requires a significant amount of time and clerical effort to enter the accounting data into the accounting software
and is also more suitable to a paralegal than a lawyer.

Ideally, the lawyer will meet with the paralegal early in the
administration of the estate or trust, review the types of receipts

and disbursements to be expected during the administration, and provide the paralegal with guidance as to how each type of asset, receipt, and disbursement will be entered including both the classification of each entry in fiduciary accounting and the description to be entered for each entry in the estate accounting software.

Sometimes accounting software causes unfamiliar transactions to appear in the printed accounting in unexpected ways. Before committing many hours to entering and updating information, it is usually a good idea to start by entering some sample information and to print an accounting to see if it looks all right.

As noted in Chapter 7, accountings should be maintained and updated throughout the administration of the estate and trust, and the lawyer should review interim accountings on a monthly or quarterly basis to compare the balances shown on the accountings and to check that the paralegal has not made any mistakes or mishandled client funds in any way.

Tax Returns

As with fiduciary accounting, the mechanics of tax return preparation can also be completed by a paralegal if adequate guidance is given by the lawyer. If a fiduciary accounting is prepared before a death tax return or income tax return is prepared, the lawyer should be able to review the accounting with the paralegal and give specific instructions about how the various items should be reported on the return, what tax elections should be made, and what information is needed from outside the accounting (or outside the probate estate) to prepare a complete and accurate return.

Associates

Unfortunately, it is often difficult to train an associate lawyer in an estates practice. Training associates, and the effective and economical use of associates, presents a number of problems.

The preceding sections of this chapter discuss lawyers giving guidance to paralegals. Unfortunately, you can't really tell someone else how to do something unless you know how to do it yourself, and the best way to learn how to do something is to do it.

That means that lawyers need to "get their hands dirty" and prepare accountings, tax returns, and estate planning presentations. Lawyers can't be sure that they understand all the legal and practical issues in a tax return until they themselves have gone through the return line by line. In addition, lawyers can't be sure that software works the way they want—and produces the results they want—until they themselves have used the software and checked the results.

A necessary part of training of an associate then is for the associate to do the tasks of a paralegal at least once. By giving the associate the guidance that a lawyer would give a paralegal, requiring the associate to do the work of the paralegal, and reviewing the associate's work as though it were the work of a paralegal, the associate will become familiar with the issues and problems in estate planning and administration, the procedures of the senior lawyer (and the firm), and how to use and supervise paralegals through the example of the senior lawyer. However, the law firm should not bill the client for an associate's time performing paralegal work, so the firm will lose money training the associate.

Training associates in client relations presents similar problems. An associate should attend client meetings and client interviews to learn about the issues that can arise as well as how to collect the information needed for estate planning and estate administrations. Client meetings don't really require more than one lawyer, so it may not be possible to bill the client for the associate's time. In fact, if the firm bills for estate planning on a fixed-fee basis, as suggested in Chapter 4, the additional associate time will almost never result in increased revenues. So the law firm will lose money training the associate in client meetings.

Once the law firm spends all this time and money training the associate, what will the associate do? The answer is usually that the associate will work on simpler estate plans and simpler administrations and assist the senior lawyer in researching and resolving more complex issues for more complex estate plans as well as the occasional drafting problem not easily solved by existing forms. Using a system of fixed fees, the firm should be able to charge the same fees for the associate's work on the simpler estates as would have been charged by the senior lawyer, and the firm should make a profit on the difference between the associate's compensation and the senior lawyer's compensation. The senior lawyer should then be able to spend more time on larger, more complex estates, which presumably will result in larger fees and so compensate the senior lawyer and the firm.

These considerations show that the expense of training an associate may be considerably more than the expense of training a secretary, paralegal, or other employee. The decision to take on a new associate should only be made when the firm has an expected volume of work that the associate will be able to assume fairly quickly with minimal supervision, freeing senior lawyers to do more highly compensated work.

Other Employees

A larger firm may require a number of other kinds of employees to operate efficiently. Larger numbers of receipts and disbursements may require the services of a full-time bookkeeper or even an entire accounting department. Maintenance of the computer network, as well as the number of people needing technical support or training, may make it necessary to have an information systems specialist. Librarians can do more than manage books. They can be valuable research assistants, particularly in emerging areas like finding cases, statutes, and other information on the Internet. While a small firm would not require such specialization, a larger firm can combine the needs of enough lawyers to make that kind of assistance cost-effective. In addition, an office manager may be needed to take care of the paperwork required by all of these employees, as well as to deal with supplies, office maintenance, and other management responsibilities.

The Contractor Option

In considering the tasks that need to be performed in your office and the people you will need for those tasks, don't overlook the possibility of hiring independent contractors to work in (or even outside of) your office, for part of each week or as needed. Some types of work that can be performed outside of the firm, and types of independent contractors to perform the work, include the following:

- ◆ Fiduciary accounting, tax returns, and other paralegal tasks can sometimes be contracted out to accountants or independent paralegals with the right experience and qualifications.
- ◆ Secretarial services can obtained on a part-time or independent contractor basis, which may be appropriate when occasional help is needed for filing or file management, data entry, or other clerical tasks not requiring a paralegal.
- ◆ Lawyers can sometimes be engaged as independent contractors and serve some of the functions of associates. They can be useful in specific legal research projects and in drafting and reviewing client documents.
- ◆ Many smaller firms do not need a full-time bookkeeper, computer systems administrator, librarian, or other administrative service person but can still obtain the needed services part-time through an independent contractor.

Ethics Compliance

A final consideration here is that every partner (or supervising lawyer) is required to make reasonable efforts to ensure that the firm's lawyers (or subordinate lawyers) conform to the rules of professional conduct. In addition, every partner in a law firm is required to make reasonable efforts to ensure that the conduct of non-lawyer employees or assistants is compatible with the lawyer's professional obligations. See Rules 5.1 and 5.3 of the *Model Rules of Professional Conduct.* This means that it is not enough that a lawyer keep a client's confidences. The lawyer's staff also must keep those confidences, and the lawyer is responsible for instructing the staff in those ethical obligations and taking reasonable steps to confirm their compliance.

Appendix A

GENERAL FEE AGREEMENT

[The following is a form of fee agreement for services for which a fixed fee could not be determined and which will therefore be billed at hourly rates. (Compare Appendices B and C.)]

When possible, the preparation of documents, tax returns, and other specific services will be billed at a fixed fee negotiated in advance of the performance of services. When it is not possible to fix a fee in advance, fees will be determined on the basis of time spent and the following billing rates:

Services	Fees
Legal and tax research, analysis, and advice; representation in court and before tax or governmental authorities; communications or negotiations with adverse parties; and similar legal services	$XXX/hour
Client meetings, telephone conferences, and correspondence	$XXX/hour
Accounting, financial calculations, tax return preparation, and other administrative services	$XX/hour
Extraordinary copying costs (not correspondence or tax returns), database services, long-distance telephone charges, travel expenses, and other direct costs incurred	At cost

Statements will be issued monthly, and all statements will be payable on receipt. Any balance not paid within one month of billing will be subject to interest at 1 percent per month, compounded monthly. Payment in advance may be required for filing fees, court costs, and other extraordinary costs.

The undersigned agrees to this fee schedule and billing procedure.

Date: _____   Signature: _____

Appendix B

ESTATE PLANNING FEE AGREEMENT

[The following is a form of fee agreement that can be used to set a fixed fee for document preparation or other estate planning services after an initial consultation. The provisions at the end of this appendix, which are normally printed on the reverse side of the agreement, are intended to avoid some of the ethical uncertainties described in Chapter 3.]

It is agreed that the documents discussed during the initial consultation, and any other services described below, shall be prepared or performed in consideration of the fees set forth below. If additional services are requested, a reasonable fee will be assessed based on time spent and costs incurred, in accordance with the hourly rates described below. In all cases, charges may be added for unusual copying, postage, and other costs.

Preparation of Documents	Fees
Will(s)/Revocable trust(s)	
Including: marital deduction formula/marital trust/unified credit trust/trusts for children/ other trusts/other provisions	
Irrevocable trust for life insurance	
Irrevocable trust(s) for gifts to children	
Durable powers of attorney(s)	
Advance health care declaration(s)	

Other Services (Describe)

Additional Services and Costs	Basis for Fees
Legal and tax research, tax calculations, analysis, and advice on any other matters	$XXX/hour
Client meetings, telephone conferences, and nonroutine correspondence not included in document preparation fees or other services described above	$XXX/hour
Extraordinary copying (not correspondence or tax returns), database services, long-distance telephone charges, travel expenses, or other costs incurred	At cost

The fees for the preparation of documents shall include corrections and revisions, telephone conversations necessary to complete the documents, and a meeting to review and execute them, but shall not include (1) additional consultations on other issues, (2) change of beneficiary designations of life insurance policies or of retirement benefits, or (3) change of ownership of life insurance policies or other assets, although general advice and forms will be supplied.

Fees for documents may be billed after initial drafts have been delivered. All statements of fees and costs shall be payable on receipt, and any balance not paid within one month of billing shall be subject to interest at 1 percent per month.

By their signatures below, the undersigned agree(s) to this fee schedule and billing procedure and also confirm that they have read and agree to the provisions on the reverse side regarding the ethical obligations of the attorney and the undersigned.

Date: _____   Signature: _____

_____

[Name of Firm] ("the attorneys") and the individual or individuals who have signed this agreement on the reverse side ("the clients") also agree as follows:

Obligations of Attorneys

1. The clients have or will communicate to the attorneys information about their finances, families, and estate planning goals that they expect will be kept confidential, and the attorneys shall keep those communications confidential and shall not disclose those communications to any other person without the consent of the clients or either of them.
2. Although the attorneys may from time to time in the future send the clients newsletters or other information about changes in tax or other laws relevant to the clients' estate planning, the attorneys have no obligation to notify the clients of any future change in any law, or of any other circumstance that might affect their estate planning.
3. The attorneys shall use their best efforts to prepare documents and recommendations to carry out the estate planning goals of the clients, but do not guarantee any particular tax or other result.
4. The attorneys may have other legal or ethical obligations to the clients, none of which are waived by this agreement.

Obligations of Clients

1. The clients agree that the information they provide to the attorneys shall be accurate, and that the attorneys shall have no obligation to verify any information provided by them.
2. The clients have provided to the attorneys all of the information requested by the attorneys and all of the information which the clients believe to be relevant to their estate plans, and the clients agree that the attorneys shall have no responsibility for any consequence of incomplete or inaccurate information.

Consents to Family Representation

1. If the clients are husband and wife (or other life partners), it is agreed that the attorneys shall be representing and advising each of them separately, and not jointly or in common, even though the clients will meet with the attorneys together and will be charged one fee for the attorneys' services. Although husbands and wives sometimes have different plans for their assets during their lifetimes and different goals for the disposition of their assets after death, the clients agree that there is no conflict between them and that the attorneys may represent and advise both of them without any prejudice to them. As a result:

   a. It is understood that there may be no attorney-client privilege for communications between the two clients, or between the client and the attorneys in the presence of another client, and that, in the event of a future dispute between the clients, the attorneys may be required to testify as to their conversations in the attorneys' presence.

   b. It is agreed that the attorneys shall have no obligation to either client to disclose any confidential communication from the other client, even if the communication is relevant to the estate planning decisions of the other client.

   c. It is agreed that, following the termination of the representation, even if owing to a dispute between the clients, the attorneys may continue to represent either or both of the clients separately, but may not represent either client in any matter that is adverse to the other client unless otherwise allowed by law or rule of court.

Appendix C

AN ESTATE ADMINISTRATION FEE AGREEMENT

[The following is a form of fee agreement that can be used to set fixed fees for specific tasks in an estate administration, as suggested in Chapter 4.]

When possible, routine services and tax returns are billed on a per-item or per-transaction basis, providing for greater certainty in the determination of fees. Questions involving unusual assets, unusual will or trust provisions, and the advisability of different tax elections may require legal services billed at hourly rates.

Services	Fees
Preparation and filing of petition for probate of will, application for employer identification number, notice of fiduciary relationship, notices to beneficiaries, and advertisement of letters	$XXX Plus $XX for each notice to a beneficiary
Accounting for receipts and disbursements of estate	$XXX base fee Plus $XX for each original asset Plus $X for every other transaction
Preparation and filing of estate inventory	$XXX base fee Plus $X for each asset included in inventory
Preparation and filing of federal estate tax return (if needed)	$XXX base fee Plus $X for each probate asset or deduction reported on return Plus $XX for each non-probate asset or deduction reported on return Plus $X for each page of attachments

Preparation and filing of applicable state inheritance tax return	$XXX base fee Plus $X for each probate asset or deduction reported on return Plus $XX for each non-probate asset or deduction reported on return Plus $X for each page of attachments
Preparation and filing of federal gift tax return (if needed)	$XXX base fee Plus $XX for each gift reported Plus $X for each page of attachments
Preparation of receipts from beneficiaries of estate (if needed)	$XX per receipt
Preparation of standard form of family agreement in final settlement of estate among adult beneficiaries (if needed)	$XXX
Legal and tax research, analysis, and advice on any matters unusual to estate, including any questions regarding rights of beneficiaries, tax or legal consequences of estate and trust distributions, tax basis of assets, choice of tax year, apportionment of death taxes, disclaimers, nonmarketable stock or partnership interests, contract rights, rights in trusts, and other unusual assets or liabilities, as well as court appearances and representation in tax disputes	$XXX/hour
Client meetings, telephone conferences, and substantive correspondence with the executors, beneficiaries, or other interested parties	$XXX/hour
Bookkeeping, factual research, and other clerical services	$XX/hour
Extraordinary copying (not correspondence or tax returns), database services, long-distance telephone charges, travel expenses, or other costs incurred	At cost

The estate will be responsible for all filing fees, taxes, appraisals, and other expenses of administration.

The above fees are based on the assumption that all information necessary to the preparation of tax returns (including appraisals and valuations of assets) will be supplied by the client, and time needed to collect or verify information may be billed at the lowest hourly rate shown above. Some of the tasks covered by fixed fees will require cover letters or other correspondence, such as notices required by law or the transmittal of tax returns, and those communications are included in the fees for those tasks. Other communications with the executors, beneficiaries, or other interested parties, including meetings, telephone conferences, and correspondence, will be billed at the hourly rate shown above.

Statements will be issued not less frequently than quarterly, and all statements will be payable on receipt. Any balance not paid within one month of billing will be subject to interest at 1 percent per month. All base fees for services to be completed in the first nine months of estate will be billed, in advance, in three quarterly installments, and all costs and all other fees will be billed when incurred.

The undersigned executor agrees to this fee schedule and billing procedure.

Executor of the Estate of _____

Appendix D

ESTATE PLANNING QUESTIONNAIRE

PERSONAL AND FAMILY INFORMATION

Husband's Name: _____

Date of Birth: _____ Citizenship: _____

Home Address: _____

City, State, Zip: _____ Telephone No.: _____

Husband's Occupation: _____ Soc. Sec. No.: _____

Name of Employer: _____

Business Address: _____

City, State, Zip: _____ Telephone No.: _____

Wife's Name: _____

Date of Birth: _____ Citizenship: _____

Home Address: _____

City, State, Zip: _____ Telephone No.: _____

Wife's Occupation: _____ Soc. Sec. No.: _____

Name of Employer: _____

Business Address: _____

City, State, Zip: _____ Telephone No.: _____

Children or Other Beneficiaries:

Name	Relationship	Date of Birth	Soc. Sec. No.

ASSETS AND LIABILITIES
(Rounded to nearest thousands)

Assets	Total Values Owned By		
	Husband	**Wife**	**Jointly**
Cash (bank accounts, certificates of deposit)	$_____	$_____	$_____
Marketable securities (stocks and bonds)	$_____	$_____	$_____
Notes and receivables (money owed to you)	$_____	$_____	$_____
Businesses you own	$_____	$_____	$_____
Home (list mortgage below)	$_____	$_____	$_____
Other real estate (list mortgages below)	$_____	$_____	$_____
Insurance on husband's life (face amount)	$_____	$_____	$_____
Insurance on wife's life (face amount)	$_____	$_____	$_____
Retirement plans (death benefits)	$_____	$_____	$_____
Furniture and furnishings	$_____	$_____	$_____
Other personal property (cars, jewelry, etc.)	$_____	$_____	$_____
Other assets (not described above)	$_____	$_____	$_____
TOTAL ASSETS	$_____	$_____	$_____

Liabilities	Total Amounts Owed By		
	Husband	**Wife**	**Jointly**
Mortgage on home	$_____	$_____	$_____
Mortgage on other real property	$_____	$_____	$_____
Loans against life insurance	$_____	$_____	$_____
Other debts	$_____	$_____	$_____
TOTAL LIABILITIES	$_____	$_____	$_____
Net Worths	$_____	$_____	$_____
Combined Net Worth			$_____

DEATH BENEFITS
(Life insurance and retirement plans)

Name of Policy or Plan[1]	Death Benefit	Present Value[2]	Beneficiary
_____	$_____	$_____	_____
_____	$_____	$_____	_____
_____	$_____	$_____	_____
_____	$_____	$_____	_____
_____	$_____	$_____	_____
_____	$_____	$_____	_____
_____	$_____	$_____	_____
_____	$_____	$_____	_____
_____	$_____	$_____	_____
_____	$_____	$_____	_____
_____	$_____	$_____	_____
_____	$_____	$_____	_____
_____	$_____	$_____	_____
_____	$_____	$_____	_____

[1] For life insurance policies, give the name of the insurance company, the policy number, and the type of insurance (i.e., term, whole life, universal life, etc.). For retirement plans and other employment benefits, give the name of the plan and the type of plan (i.e., qualified pension plan, qualified profit-sharing plan, nonqualified pension plan, stock option plan, etc.).

[2] For life insurance policies, give the present cash surrender value of the policy, if known. For many retirement plans, the value of the death benefit may be the same as the present value of accrued benefits.

OTHER INFORMATION

(These questions apply to both husband and wife.)

1. Please supply copies of your present wills, any trusts you have created (revocable or irrevocable), any declarations regarding medical treatment (living wills), and any "durable" powers of attorney.

2. If you have ever filed any gift tax returns, please supply copies of those returns.

3. If you hold any accounts or own any property jointly with anyone other than your husband or wife, please describe the property, the nature of your interest, and the names of the co-owners.

_____

_____

_____

4. If you own a business (and for each business you own), respond to questions 5–7:

5. Please supply a copy of the most recent financial statement for the business.

6. If your business is a partnership, what is your interest and who are the other partners? If it is a corporation, how much and what kind of stock is outstanding and who owns it (and in what amounts)? _____

_____

_____

7. If there is a partnership or shareholder agreement, please supply a copy of the agreement.

8. If you have a written employment agreement with any corporation, please supply a copy of the agreement.

9. Are you entitled to receive the income or principal from any existing trust or estate? Please describe your interest:_____

_____

_____

10. Do you expect to inherit any property from anyone else? ___

_____

11. If you have been married before, please provide the name of your previous husband or wife and the date of the death or divorce:

12. If you are obliged to provide in your will for, or support during your lifetime, your former husband or wife or any children from a previous marriage, please supply a copy of your divorce agreement or decree.

13. If you have signed a premarital agreement, please supply a copy.

14. Are you under any other obligation to leave any part of your estate to any particular person or in any particular way? ___

_____

15. Please supply the names and addresses of your accountant, insurance agent, and any other tax or investment advisors.

_____

_____

_____

Appendix E

DRAFTING INSTRUCTIONS FOR ESTATE PLANNING DOCUMENTS

[This is a sample of a form that can be used to memorialize the drafting instructions for a client's estate planning documents. It might be used to record decisions during an estate planning client interview, or to communicate instructions to a paralegal who will be drafting the documents. This form has been reproduced by permission of Edward R. Parker of Parker, Pollard & Brown, P.C., of Richmond, Virginia.]

Name: _____ (file to be opened) ❏ Yes ❏ No

How did you learn about PP&B?

a. ___ Television Advertising   g. ___ *Hanover Press*

b. ___ WRVA Law Line Show   h. ___ Former Client

c. ___ Yellow Pages   i. ___ Legal Resources, Inc.

d. ___ Referral   j. ___ Seminar

e. ___ *Far West End Press*   k. ___ Other (please explain)

f. ___ *Chesterfield Press*

1. **Tangible Personal Property**
   a. Specific Bequests

Item	Primary Beneficiary	Contingency Beneficiary Issue
_____	_____	_____
_____	_____	_____
_____	_____	_____

b. General Bequest
  i. _____ Spouse, then living children and share to issue of deceased children
  ii. _____ Children, then descendants
  iii. _____ General bequest to individuals and descendants

_____

_____

c. TPP Memorandum
  i. _____ Discretionary
  ii. _____ Mandatory

2. *Intangible Personal Property and Real Estate*
  a. Specific Bequests

Item	Primary Beneficiary	Contingency Beneficiary Issue or Lapse
_____	_____	_____
_____	_____	_____
_____	_____	_____

b. Residuary
  i. _____ Spouse, then living children, and share for descendants
  ii. _____ Children, then descendants
  iii. _____ Named individuals and descendants

_____

_____

  iv. _____ Trust
  v. _____ Takers in Default
      Heirs at Law _____
      Other _____

_____

3. *Type of Will*

   Simple _____
   Disclaimer   Spouse ( )
                Child(ren) ( ) _____
   Pour Over _____
   All to Spouse, then Trust _____

4. *Type of Trust*

Testamentary	Revocable Inter vivos	Joint	Irrevocable	Special Needs	Charitable
_____	_____	____	_____	_____	_____

   i.   Marital
        (1) Outright _____
        (2) Trust _____
             (a) 5 & 5 _____
             (b) P/A _____
             (c) Q-TIP _____
   ii. Family
        (1) 5 & 5 _____ P/A _____
        (2) Require all income be paid out _____
        (3) Sprinkle income and principal _____
        (4) Division date: _____
        (5) Payout _____ _____ _____
   iii. Takers in Default
        (1) _____ Heirs at Law
        (2) _____ Other _____
             _____

5. *Executors*
   a.   _____ Spouse as Executor
   b.   _____ Other _____
   c.   _____ Substitute _____

d. _____ Compensation

Yes	No	Reasonable	Fee Schedule	Spouse	Others
___	___	___	___	___	___

6. ***Trustee*** _____
   Substitute Trustee _____

   Compensation

Yes	No	Reasonable	Fee Schedule	Spouse	Others
___	___	___	___	___	___

7. ***Fiduciary letter sent if PP&B named as Executor/Trustee:***
   ❏ Yes

8. ***Forfeiture Clause Upon Contest of Will:*** ❏ Yes ❏ No

9. ***General Power of Attorney:*** ❏ Yes ❏ No
   a. Agent
   b. Substitute
   Revoke Previous POA: ❏ Yes ❏ No **Record:** ❏ Yes ❏ No

   Include Following Powers:
   Gifts: ❏ Yes ❏ No Limited _____ Unlimited _____
   Compensation: ❏ Yes ❏ No
   Health Care Provisions: ❏ Yes ❏ No

10. ***Advance Medical Directive*** ❏ Yes ❏ No
    a. Direction as to **Anatomical Gifts.** (Initial only one)
       i. _____ My agent may make anatomical gifts of part or all of my body for medical purposes, authorize an autopsy, and direct the disposition of my remains to the extent permitted by law.
       ii. _____ Omit language about anatomical gifts.

b. Directions as to **Life-Sustaining Treatment** (Initial only one of the following paragraphs)

    i. ____ Reference to Living Will. I specifically direct my Agent to follow any health care declaration or *living will* executed by me.

    ii. ____ Grant of Discretion to Agent. I do not want my life to be prolonged nor do I want life-sustaining treatment to be provided or continued if my Agent believes the burdens of the treatment outweigh the expected benefits. I want my Agent to consider the relief of suffering, the expense involved, and the quality as well as the possible extension of my life in making decisions concerning life-sustaining treatment.

    iii. ____ Directive to Withhold or Withdraw Treatment. I do not want my life to be prolonged and I do not want life-sustaining treatment:

        (1) if I have a condition that is incurable or irreversible and, without the administration of life-sustaining treatment, expected to result in death within a relatively short time; or

        (2) if I am in a coma or persistent vegetative state which is reasonably concluded to be irreversible.

    iv. ____ Directive for Maximum Treatment. I want my life to be prolonged to the greatest extent possible without regard to my condition, the chances I have for recovery, or the cost of the procedures.

    v. ____ Directive in My Own Words: _____

_____

_____

_____

c. Direction as to **Nutrition and Hydration** provided by means of a nasogastric tube or tube into the stomach, intestines, or veins. (Initial only one)

    i. ____ I *intend* to include these procedures among the life-sustaining procedures that may be withheld or withdrawn under the conditions given above.

ii. _____ I *do not intend* to include these procedures among the life-sustaining procedures that may be withheld or withdrawn.

d. Agent authorized to enter Do Not Resuscitate Order.
❏ Yes ❏ No

e. Agent: _____
Address: _____
_____
Telephone: (Home) _____ (Office) _____

f. Alternate Agent: _____
Address: _____
_____
Telephone: (Home) _____ (Office) _____

g. Second Alternate Agent: _____
Address: _____
_____
Telephone: (Home) _____ (Office) _____

11. ***Guardian Letter*** ❏ Yes ❏ No Guardian _____
Substitute _____

12. ***Deed of Gift:*** ❏ Yes ❏ No TC___ Sole Name of _____
Record: ❏ Yes ❏ No

13. ***Appointment Date:*** _____ Time _____
a. To sign all documents _____
b. To discuss alternatives _____
c. Other _____

14. ***Second Appointment Date:*** _____ Time _____
a. To sign all documents _____
b. To discuss alternatives _____
c. Other _____

15. ***To Meet with Client:*** Attorney _____ BGS _____ PAP _____

16. ***Date to Enter on Master Calendar*** _____

17. ***Fee*** $ _____ Pay At Signing: ❏ Yes ❏ No

18. ***Custodian of Will:*** ❏ PP&B ❏ Client

19. ***Custodian of General P/A***: ❏ PP&B ❏ Client

20. ***Name entered on GST database*** _____

Appendix F

ESTATE AND PROBATE INFORMATION

[The following is a form that can be used to collect personal information about a decedent and the estate beneficiaries for an estate administration, either by sending the form to the client or by using it as a checklist during a client meeting.]

To complete the petition for probate, tax returns, and other forms necessary for the administration of an estate, the following information will be needed:

Decedent's Name: _____

Date of Birth: _____ Citizenship: _____

Date of Death: _____ Place of Death: _____

Home Address: _____

City, State, Zip: _____ Year Domicile Est.: _____

Decedent's Occupation: _____ Soc. Sec. No.: _____

Name of Employer: _____

Employer's Address: _____

City, State, Zip: _____ Telephone No.: _____

Spouse's Name: _____

Date of Birth: _____ Citizenship: _____

Telephone No.: _____ Soc. Sec. No.: _____

Children and Other Beneficiaries:

Name and Address	Relationship	Date of Birth	Soc. Sec. No.
_____	_____	_____	_____
_____	_____	_____	_____
_____	_____	_____	_____
_____	_____	_____	_____

Appendix G

ESTATE ADMINISTRATION CHECKLIST

[The following is an example of instructions that can be given to a client who wishes to collect the information needed to prepare the inventory, tax returns, and other reports required in an estate administration.]

To complete the tax returns and other transactions necessary for the administration of an estate, the following information will be needed.

I. ESTATE ASSETS—For each asset in the name of the decedent at death:
   A. Real Estate—For each parcel of real estate:
      1. A copy of the last real estate tax bill or tax assessment.
      2. If there is no street address, a copy of the deed to the property.
      3. A professional appraisal (or, in the case of property owned jointly by husband and wife, a letter of value from a real estate agent).
   B. Bank Deposits—For each bank account or bank certificate of deposit, a letter from the bank stating:
      1. The name of the bank.
      2. The account number.
      3. The name (or names) appearing on the account.
      4. The balance of the account upon the date of death.
      5. The amount of interest accrued to the date of death, but not yet credited.
   C. Stocks—For each publicly traded stock:
      1. The name of the issuing corporation.
      2. The class of stock (i.e., common or preferred).
      3. The number of shares held at death.
      4. The CUSIP number and "ticker symbol" for the security.

     5. The fair market value of the shares on the date of death.[1]

     6. If the stock was "ex dividend" on the date of death, the amount of the dividend.[2]

  D. Bonds and Notes—For each publicly traded bond or note:

     1. The name of the issuing corporation, government, or authority.

     2. The face amount of the bond or note.

     3. The date of issue and date of maturity.

     4. The stated rate of interest.

     5. The CUSIP number for the bond or note.

     6. The fair market value of the bond or note on the date of death.[3]

     7. The amount of unpaid interest accrued to the date of death.

  E. Closely Held Businesses—For each private corporation or partnership in which the decedent had an interest:

     1. Copies of financial statements for each of the five fiscal years preceding the date of death and a financial statement for the year of death as soon as it is available.

     2. A copy of any shareholder agreement or partnership agreement.

     3. If the corporation or partnership owns real estate or equipment that may have appreciated in value, it may be necessary to obtain an appraisal of the properties.

  F. Other Notes—For each note or mortgage for which no market exists:

     1. The name of the maker of the note or mortgage.

---

1. For tax purposes, the fair market value is the average of the highest and lowest selling prices on the death of death. If there were no transactions in a security on the date of death, please provide the average of the highest and lowest selling prices on the last day before the date of death and on the first day after the date of death for which there were transactions, together with the respective dates of the transactions.

2. A stock may be "ex dividend" if a dividend is declared before the date of death but the dividend is payable to shareholders of record after the date of death.

3. See note 1, above. If market prices are not readily available, a broker's opinion of value should be sufficient.

2. The face amount of the note or mortgage.
3. The date of the note or mortgage and the date of maturity.
4. The stated rate of interest.
5. The amount of unpaid interest accrued to the date of death.
6. A description of the security for the note or the property subject to the mortgage.
7. Any other information relevant to the fair market value of the note or mortgage, such as a history of defaults or late payments, the value of the security, or the creditworthiness of the maker.

G. Tangible Personal Property—An appraisal of household furniture, furnishings, jewelry, silver, china, appliances, automobiles, and other personal effects is recommended, particularly if there are items of particular value (e.g., antiques, fine art, or collections).

II. ASSETS JOINTLY OWNED WITH HUSBAND OR WIFE—In Pennsylvania, all assets in the names of both husband and wife are presumed to be owned as tenants by the entireties and so pass automatically to the surviving spouse. However, one half of those assets are still included in the gross estate for federal estate tax purposes, and so the same information will be needed as for assets in the name of the decedent alone. (See Part I above.)

III. ASSETS JOINTLY OWNED WITH OTHERS—Assets in the names of the decedent and one or more persons other than a surviving spouse may pass automatically to the surviving co-owners if the surviving co-owners have rights of survivorship. However, the entire value of an asset will be subject to federal estate tax unless the surviving owners can prove that they contributed to the purchase of the asset. Therefore, the same information is needed for jointly owned assets as for assets in the decedent's name alone (see Part I above) and the following additional information will be required:

A. A copy of the title to each asset should be provided so that it can be determined if the asset passes to the co-owners or is part of the estate that passes under the will.

B. For federal estate tax purposes, please provide whatever evidence is available to show the contribution of each surviving owner to the purchase of the property.

C. For Pennsylvania inheritance tax purposes, please identify each asset transferred from the name of the decedent into joint names within one year of death.

IV. GIFTS—For federal gift tax purposes, the following information will be needed with respect to each gift of the decedent made in the year of death. For Pennsylvania inheritance tax purposes, the following information will be needed for each gift within one year of death to the extent that the total of the gifts to one recipient exceeded $3,000:

A. Name, address, and Social Security number of the recipient.

B. Date of gift.

C. Amount or description of gift. If gift was in property, the description should include the same information as that required above for an asset of the estate, including the fair market value on the date of the gift.

V. LIFE INSURANCE—For each policy of insurance on the life of the decedent, a Form 712 will be needed from the insurer.

VI. RETIREMENT BENEFITS AND ANNUITIES—If any amount is payable to the estate or any beneficiary by reason of the decedent's death under any pension or profit-sharing plan, individual retirement account, stock option plan, annuity contract, employment agreement, or other arrangement, please provide:

A. A description of the plan, contract, or other arrangement.

B. The name, address, and Social Security number of the beneficiary.

C. The amount payable to the recipient as of the decedent's death.

VII. ESTATE RECEIPTS—For each cash receipt after the date of death, either in the name of the decedent or in the name of the estate of the decedent:

A. The name of the payor.

B. The amount of the payment.

C. The date of the check.

D. The date received or deposited.

E. A brief explanation of the reason for the receipt (i.e., dividend, insurance refund, or such) or a copy of the disbursement memo, letter, or other documentation accompanying the receipt.

VIII. ESTATE DISBURSEMENTS—For each cash disbursement from the estate, and for any payment after death for any medical expenses of the decedent, any funeral expenses, legal expenses, accounting expenses, debts (including taxes) in the name of the decedent, or other expenses incurred by reason of the death of the decedent or in connection with the property of the decedent:

A. The name of the payee.

B. The amount of the payment.

C. The date of the check.

D. A brief explanation of the reason for the payment (i.e., debt, expense, or such) or a copy of the invoice or bill being paid.

IX. ESTATE BENEFICIARIES—Please provide the name, address, and Social Security number of each beneficiary of the estate. If any beneficiary is a minor (i.e., under the age of eighteen), please provide the minor's birth date.

X. OTHER INFORMATION—Please also provide copies of:

A. The last federal and state income tax returns filed by the decedent.

B. The last personal property tax return filed by the decedent.

C. Any trusts created by the decedent during his or her lifetime.

D. Any gift tax returns filed by the decedent.

E. Any trusts in which the decedent had any interest.

F. If the decedent was divorced, a copy of the divorce decree and separation agreement (or supply the name of the previous husband or wife and the date of the death or divorce).

G. Any premarital agreement entered into by the decedent.

H. The names and addresses of the decedent's accountant, insurance agent, stock broker, and any other tax or investment advisors.

Appendix H

ESTATE ADMINISTRATION SCHEDULE

[The following is an example of a schedule that can be given to an estate executor or administrator or other client interested in estate administration to provide general information about estate administrations.]

The following is a general description of the steps, and the timing of the steps, usually needed for the administration of an estate.

I. GENERAL DUTIES—The general duties of an executor or administrator of an estate are to:
    A. Collect the assets of the estate.
    B. Pay debts and taxes owed by the decedent or the estate.
    C. Distribute the estate in accordance with the will (or, if there is no will, in accordance with the laws of intestacy).

II. INITIAL TASKS—Shortly after death, it is usually necessary to:
    A. Arrange for the funeral (if there is no surviving husband or wife, children, or other next of kin).
    B. If there is an unoccupied residence, make sure that it and any valuables in or around it are secure.
    C. Arrange for the probate of the will (or the grant of letters of administration if there is no will) with the register of wills.

III. WITHIN THREE MONTHS OF DEATH
    A. Notify banks, employers, insurance companies, stock brokers, and others of the death, and begin identifying assets and liabilities of the decedent. (See separate checklist for information to be collected.) [Refer to the "Estate Administration Checklist" in Appendix G.]
    B. If appropriate, arrange for the decedent's mail to be forwarded.
    C. Advertise the grant of letters by the register of wills.

D. Send required written notices to beneficiaries under the will and to heirs at law, with certification to the register of wills.

E. Make advance payment of Pennsylvania inheritance tax (for discount).

IV. WITHIN SIX MONTHS OF DEATH

A. Estimate cash needed to pay debts and taxes, and plan for any sales of assets needed to distribute the estate.

B. Prepare and file inventory of the estate with the register of wills.

V. WITHIN NINE MONTHS OF DEATH

A. Prepare and file Pennsylvania inheritance tax return.

B. Prepare and file federal estate tax return (if needed).

C. Prepare and file any other death tax returns needed for property located in other states.

VI. OTHER TASKS

A. Prepare and file the decedent's final lifetime income tax returns, federal and state (due on April 15 of the year following death).

B. During the administration of an estate, federal and state income tax returns must be filed showing the income and expenses of the estate.

VII. DISTRIBUTION OF ESTATE—The distribution of assets from the estate can begin at any time but is usually concluded after the death taxes have been settled. Depending on the circumstances, distributions can be carried out:

A. After an accounting has been filed in court and approved by the court.

B. After an accounting and schedule of distribution has been approved by all beneficiaries.

C. By receipt and release from each beneficiary.

VIII. FINAL FILINGS—Once the administration of an estate has been completed and the assets have been distributed:

A. Final federal and state income tax returns may be filed.

B. Notice should be given to the register of wills through a status report.

Appendix I

WILL EXECUTION INSTRUCTIONS

[The following form can be used to instruct a client on how to execute a will outside of a lawyer's supervision.]

To: _____

Your will should be executed in the following way:

1. You should sign your will in the presence of two witnesses who are not beneficiaries under your will. (As explained below, it is also desirable, but not legally necessary, that a notary public be present.) The line for your signature has your name typed underneath, and appears on page ___.

2. You should fill in the date in the sentence above your name.

3. The two witnesses should sign and fill in their addresses on the line provided following your signature.

4. To simplify the probate of your will in the event of your death, it is desirable (but not legally necessary) to complete the affidavit that is the last page of your will. To complete the affidavit:

    a. You and the two witnesses should appear before a notary public and sign your names on the lines provided on that last page. The line for your signature has your name typed underneath and the lines for the signatures of the witnesses have "Witness" typed underneath.

    b. The notary should date, sign, and seal the affidavit. The notary should also complete the affidavit by filling in the name of the county as well as the names of the witnesses in the first and last paragraphs.

5. The executed will should be returned to me so that I can confirm that it was properly executed and make copies for our records. I can return the original to you if you wish, but I would prefer to place it in my document vault for safekeeping, where it will be more easily accessible to me and (if necessary) members of your family.

Postscript

I consider an estates practice to be one of the most challenging legal practices, and some of the discussions in this book may help to illustrate why.

Estate planning and administration are technically challenging, often requiring an understanding of not only difficult provisions of the Internal Revenue Code and regulations, but also state laws relating to estates, trusts, and property rights and economic and financial principles relating to investments and the consequences of the timing of receipts and disbursements.

At the other end of the spectrum of practice skills, an estates practice can be emotionally challenging, requiring an ability to deal with people in great personal distress due to the death or disability of a family member, as well as family conflicts.

And an estates practice requires management skills, due to the special problems of marketing and supervising a practice that demands both efficiency and individual attention to the needs of clients.

As I said in the Introduction, this is a book of ideas, and I hope it has given you some new ideas about your own practice. If you can find a new marketing idea, a new niche for your practice, a new way of pricing your services, a new form to use to communicate with your clients, or a new way of dealing with particular types of tasks or clients, you should be able to make your practice more efficient and more enjoyable.

The goal is not perfection, but progress, and I hope that this book has contributed to the progress of your estates practice.

Index

Selected Books From . . .
THE ABA LAW PRACTICE MANAGEMENT SECTION

The ABA Guide to International Business Negotiations. Explains national, legal, and cultural issues you must consider when negotiating with members of different countries. Includes details of 17 specific countries/nationalities.

The ABA Guide to Lawyer Trust Accounts. Details ways that lawyers should manage trust accounts to comply with ethical & statutory requirements.

The ABA Guide to Legal Marketing. 14 articles—written by marketing experts, practicing lawyers, and law firm marketing administrators—share their innovative methods for competing in an aggressive marketplace.

The ABA Guide to Professional Managers in the Law Office. Shows how lawyers can practice more efficiently by delegating management tasks to professional managers.

Anatomy of a Law Firm Merger. Considering a merger? Here's a roadmap that shows how to: determine the costs/benefits of a merger, assess merger candidates, integrate resources and staff, and more.

Billing Innovations. Explains how billing and pricing are affect strategic planning, maintaining quality of services, marketing, instituting a compensation system, and firm governance.

Changing Jobs, 3rd Edition. A handbook designed to help lawyers make changes in their professional careers. Includes career planning advice from dozens of experts.

Compensation Plans for Law Firms, 2nd Ed. This second edition discusses the basics for a fair and simple compensation system for partners, of counsel, associates, paralegals, and staff.

The Complete Internet Handbook for Lawyers. A thorough orientation to the Internet, including e-mail, search engines, conducting research and marketing on the Internet, publicizing a Web site, Net ethics, security, viruses, and more. Features a updated, companion Web site with forms you can download and customize.

Computer-Assisted Legal Research: A Guide to Successful Online Searching. Covers the fundamentals of LEXIS®-NEXIS® and WESTLAW®, including practical information such as: logging on and off; formulating your search; reviewing results; modifying a query; using special features; downloading documents.

Computerized Case Management Systems. Thoroughly evaluates 35 leading case management software applications, helping you pick which is best for your firm.

Connecting with Your Client. Written by a psychologist, therapist, and legal consultant, this book presents communications techniques that will help ensure client cooperation and satisfaction.

Do-It-Yourself Public Relations. A hands-on guide (and diskette!) for lawyers with public relations ideas, sample letters, and forms.

Easy Self-Audits for the Busy Law Office. Dozens of evaluation tools help you determine what's working (and what's not) in your law office or legal department. You'll discover several opportunities for improving productivity and efficiency along the way!

Finding the Right Lawyer. Answers the questions people should ask when searching for legal counsel. Includes a glossary of legal specialties and the 10 questions to ask before hiring a lawyer.

Flying Solo: A Survival Guide for the Solo Lawyer, 2nd Ed. An updated guide to the issues unique to the solo practitioner.

Handling Personnel Issues in the Law Office. Packed with tips on "safely" and legally recruiting, hiring, training, managing, and terminating employees.

HotDocs® in One Hour for Lawyers. Offers simple instructions, ranging from generating a document from a template to inserting conditional text and creating custom dialogs.

How to Build and Manage an Employment Law Practice. Provides clear guidance and valuable tips for solo or small employment law practices, including preparation, marketing, accepting cases, and managing workload and finances. Includes several time-saving "fill in the blank" forms.

How to Build and Manage an Estates Law Practice. Provides the tools and guidance you'll need to start or improve an estates law practice, including

How to Build and Manage a Personal Injury Practice. Features all of the tactics, technology, and tools needed for a profitable practice, including hot to: write a sound business plan, develop a financial forecast, choose office space, market your practice, and more.

How to Draft Bills Clients Rush to Pay. Dozens of ways to draft bills that project honesty, competence, fairness and value.

How to Start and Build a Law Practice, Millennium 4th Edition. Jay Foonberg's classic guide has been completely updated and expanded! Features 128 chapters, including 30 new ones, that reveal secrets to successful planning, marketing, billing, client relations, and much more. Chock-full of forms, sample letters, and checklists, including a sample business plan, "The Foonberg Law Office Management Checklist," and more.

Internet Fact Finder for Lawyers. Shares all of the secrets, shortcuts, and realities of conducting research on the Net, including how to tap into Internet sites for investigations, depositions, and trial presentations.

Law Firm Partnership Guide: Getting Started. Examines the most important issues you must consider to ensure your partnership's success, including self-assessment, organization structure, written agreements, financing, and basic operations. Includes *A Model Partnership Agreement* on diskette.

TO ORDER CALL TOLL-FREE:
1-800-285-2221

VISIT OUR WEB SITE:
http://www.abanet.org/lpm/catalog

Law Firm Partnership Guide: Strengthening Your Firm. Addresses what to do after your firm is up and running, including how to handle: change, financial problems, governance issues, compensating firm owners, and leadership.

Law Law Law on the Internet. Presents the most influential law-related Web sites. Features Web site reviews of the *National Law Journal's 250*, so you can save time surfing the Net and quickly find the information you need.

Law Office Policy and Procedures Manual, 3rd Ed. A model for law office policies and procedures (includes diskette). Covers law office organization, management, personnel policies, financial management, technology, and communications systems.

Law Office Staff Manual for Solos and Small Firms. Use this manual as is or customize it using the book's diskette. Includes general office policies on confidentiality, employee compensation, sick leave, sexual harassment, billing, and more.

The Lawyer's Guide to Creating Web Pages. A practical guide that clearly explains HTML, covers how to design a Web site, and introduces Web-authoring tools.

The Lawyer's Guide to the Internet. A guide to what the Internet is (and isn't), how it applies to the legal profession, and the different ways it can—and should—be used.

The Lawyer's Guide to Marketing on the Internet. This book talks about the pluses and minuses of marketing on the Internet, as well as how to develop an Internet marketing plan.

The Lawyer's Quick Guide to E-Mail. Covers basic and intermediate topics, including setting up an e-mail program, sending messages, managing received messages, using mailing lists, security, and more.

The Lawyer's Quick Guide to Microsoft® Internet Explorer; The Lawyer's Quick Guide to Netscape® Navigator. These two guides de-mystify the most popular Internet browsers. Four quick and easy lessons include: Basic Navigation, Setting a Bookmark, Browsing with a Purpose, and Keeping What You Find.

The Lawyer's Quick Guide to Timeslips®. Filled with practical examples, this guide uses three short, interactive lessons to show to efficiently use Timeslips.

The Lawyer's Quick Guide to WordPerfect® 7.0/8.0 for Windows®. Covers multitasking, entering and editing text, formatting letters, creating briefs, and more. Includes a diskette with practice exercises and word templates.

Leaders' Digest: A Review of the Best Books on Leadership. This book will help you find the best books on leadership to help you achieve extraordinary and exceptional leadership skills.

Living with the Law: Strategies to Avoid Burnout and Create Balance. Examines ways to manage stress, make the practice of law more satisfying, and improve client service.

Marketing Success Stories. This collection of anecdotes provides an inside look at how successful lawyers market themselves, their practice specialties, their firms, and their profession.

Microsoft® Word for Windows® in One Hour for Lawyers. Uses four easy lessons to help you prepare, save, and edit a basic document in Word.

Practicing Law Without Clients: Making a Living as a Freelance Lawyer. Describes freelance legal researching, writing, and consulting opportunities that are available to lawyers.

Quicken® in One Hour for Lawyers. With quick, concise instructions, this book explains the basics of Quicken and how to use the program to detect and analyze financial problems.

Risk Management. Presents practical ways to asses your level of risk, improve client services, and avoid mistakes that can lead to costly malpractice claims, civil liability, or discipline. Includes Law Firm Quality/In Control (QUIC) Surveys on diskette and other tools to help you perform a self-audit.

Running a Law Practice on a Shoestring. Offers a crash course in successful entrepreneurship. Features money-saving tips on office space, computer equipment, travel, furniture, staffing, and more.

Successful Client Newsletters. Written for lawyers, editors, writers, and marketers, this book can help you to start a newsletter from scratch, redesign an existing one, or improve your current practices in design, production, and marketing.

Survival Guide for Road Warriors. A guide to using a notebook computer (laptop) and other technology to improve your productivity in your office, on the road, in the courtroom, or at home.

Telecommuting for Lawyers. Discover methods for implementing a successful telecommuting program that can lead to increased productivity, improved work product, higher revenues, lower overhead costs, and better communications. Addressing both law firms and telecommuters, this guide covers start-up, budgeting, setting policies, selecting participants, training, and technology.

Through the Client's Eyes. Includes an overview of client relations and sample letters, surveys, and self-assessment questions to gauge your client relations acumen.

Time Matters® in One Hour for Lawyers. Employs quick, easy lessons to show you how to: add contacts, cases, and notes to Time Matters; work with events and the calendar; and integrate your data into a case management system that suits your needs.

Wills, Trusts, and Technology. Reveals why you should automate your estates practice; identifies what should be automated; explains how to select the right software; and helps you get up and running with the software you select.

Win-Win Billing Strategies. Prepared by a blue-ribbon ABA task force of practicing lawyers, corporate counsel, and management consultants, this book explores what constitutes "value" and how to bill for it. You'll understand how to get fair compensation for your work and communicate and justify fees to cost-conscious clients.

Women Rainmakers' 101+ Best Marketing Tips. A collection of over 130 marketing from women rainmakers throughout the country. Features tips on image, networking, public relations, and advertising.

Year 2000 Problem and the Legal Profession. In clear, nontechnical terms, this book will help you identify, address, and meet the challenges that Y2K poses to the legal industry.

Qty	Title	LPM Price	Regular Price	Total
___	ABA Guide to International Business Negotiations (5110331)	$ 74.95	$ 84.95	$_____
___	ABA Guide to Lawyer Trust Accounts (5110374)	69.95	79.95	$_____
___	ABA Guide to Legal Marketing (5110341)	69.95	79.95	$_____
___	ABA Guide to Prof. Managers in the Law Office (5110373)	69.95	79.95	$_____
___	Anatomy of a Law Firm Merger (5110310)	24.95	29.95	$_____
___	Billing Innovations (5110366)	124.95	144.95	$_____
___	Changing Jobs, 3rd Ed.	*please call for information*		$_____
___	Compensation Plans for Lawyers, 2nd Ed. (5110353)	69.95	79.95	$_____
___	Complete Internet Handbook for Lawyers (5110413)	39.95	49.95	$_____
___	Computer-Assisted Legal Research (5110388)	69.95	79.95	$_____
___	Computerized Case Management Systems (5110409)	39.95	49.95	$_____
___	Connecting with Your Client (5110378)	54.95	64.95	$_____
___	Do-It-Yourself Public Relations (5110352)	69.95	79.95	$_____
___	Easy Self Audits for the Busy Law Firm	*please call for information*		$_____
___	Finding the Right Lawyer (5110339)	14.95	14.95	$_____
___	Flying Solo, 2nd Ed. (5110328)	29.95	34.95	$_____
___	Handling Personnel Issues in the Law Office (5110381)	59.95	69.95	$_____
___	HotDocs® in One Hour for Lawyers (5110403)	29.95	34.95	$_____
___	How to Build and Manage an Employment Law Practice (5110389)	44.95	54.95	$_____
___	How to Build and Manage an Estates Law Practice	*please call for information*		$_____
___	How to Build and Manage a Personal Injury Practice (5110386)	44.95	54.95	$_____
___	How to Draft Bills Clients Rush to Pay (5110344)	39.95	49.95	$_____
___	How to Start & Build a Law Practice, Millennium Fourth Edition (5110415)	47.95	54.95	$_____
___	Internet Fact Finder for Lawyers (5110339)	34.95	39.95	$_____
___	Law Firm Partnership Guide: Getting Started (5110363)	64.95	74.95	$_____
___	Law Firm Partnership Guide: Strengthening Your Firm (5110391)	64.95	74.95	$_____
___	Law Law Law on the Internet (5110400)	34.95	39.95	$_____
___	Law Office Policy & Procedures Manual (5110375)	99.95	109.95	$_____
___	Law Office Staff Manual for Solos & Small Firms (5110361)	49.95	59.95	$_____
___	Lawyer's Guide to Creating Web Pages (5110383)	54.95	64.95	$_____
___	Lawyer's Guide to the Internet (5110343)	24.95	29.95	$_____
___	Lawyer's Guide to Marketing on the Internet (5110371)	54.95	64.95	$_____
___	Lawyer's Quick Guide to E-Mail (5110406)	34.95	39.95	$_____
___	Lawyer's Quick Guide to Microsoft Internet® Explorer (5110392)	24.95	29.95	$_____
___	Lawyer's Quick Guide to Netscape® Navigator (5110384)	24.95	29.95	$_____
___	Lawyer's Quick Guide to Timeslips® (5110405)	34.95	39.95	$_____
___	Lawyer's Quick Guide to WordPerfect® 7.0/8.0 (5110395)	34.95	39.95	$_____
___	Leaders' Digest (5110356)	49.95	59.95	$_____
___	Living with the Law (5110379)	59.95	69.95	$_____
___	Marketing Success Stories (5110382)	79.95	89.95	$_____
___	Microsoft® Word for Windows® in One Hour for Lawyers (5110358)	19.95	29.95	$_____
___	Practicing Law Without Clients (5110376)	49.95	59.95	$_____
___	Quicken® in One Hour for Lawyers (5110380)	19.95	29.95	$_____
___	Risk Management (5610123)	69.95	79.95	$_____
___	Running a Law Practice on a Shoestring (5110387)	39.95	49.95	$_____
___	Successful Client Newsletters (5110396)	39.95	44.95	$_____
___	Survival Guide for Road Warriors (5110362)	24.95	29.95	$_____
___	Telecommuting for Lawyers (5110401)	39.95	49.95	$_____
___	Through the Client's Eyes (5110337)	69.95	79.95	$_____
___	Time Matters® in One Hour for Lawyers (5110402)	29.95	34.95	$_____
___	Wills, Trusts, and Technology (5430377)	74.95	84.95	$_____
___	Win-Win Billing Strategies (5110304)	89.95	99.95	$_____
___	Women Rainmakers' 101+ Best Marketing Tips (5110336)	14.95	19.95	$_____
___	Year 2000 Problem and the Legal Profession (5110410)	24.95	29.95	$_____

		Subtotal	$_____
		*Handling	$_____
		**Tax	$_____
		TOTAL	$_____

*Handling
$10.00–$24.99......................$3.95
$25.00–$49.99......................$4.95
$50.00+ $5.95   MD residents add 5%

**Tax
DC residents add 5.75%
IL residents add 8.75%

PAYMENT
❏ Check enclosed (to the ABA) ❏ Bill Me
❏ Visa   ❏ MasterCard   ❏ American Express

_____
Account Number   Exp. Date   Signature

Name _____ Firm _____
Address _____
City _____ State _____ Zip _____
Phone Number _____ E-Mail Address _____

Mail: ABA Publication Orders, P.O. Box 10892, Chicago, Illinois 60610-0892 ♦ Phone: (800) 285-2221 ♦ FAX: (312) 988-5568

E-Mail: abasvcctr@abanet.org ♦ Internet: http://www.abanet.org/lpm/catalog

Source Code: 22AEND499

 THE SECTION OF LAW PRACTICE MANAGEMENT

CUSTOMER COMMENT FORM

Title of Book:_____

We've tried to make this publication as useful, accurate, and readable as possible. Please take 5 minutes to tell us if we succeeded. Your comments and suggestions will help us improve our publications. Thank you!

1. How did you acquire this publication:

☐ by mail order ☐ at a meeting/convention ☐ as a gift

☐ by phone order ☐ at a bookstore ☐ don't know

☐ other: (describe) _____

Please rate this publication as follows:

	Excellent	Good	Fair	Poor	Not Applicable
Readability: Was the book easy to read and understand?	☐	☐	☐	☐	☐
Examples/Cases: Were they helpful, practical? Were there enough?	☐	☐	☐	☐	☐
Content: Did the book meet your expectations? Did it cover the subject adequately?	☐	☐	☐	☐	☐
Organization and clarity: Was the sequence of text logical? Was it easy to find what you wanted to know?	☐	☐	☐	☐	☐
Illustrations/forms/checklists: Were they clear and useful? Were there enough?	☐	☐	☐	☐	☐
Physical attractiveness: What did you think of the appearance of the publication (typesetting, printing, etc.)?	☐	☐	☐	☐	☐

Would you recommend this book to another attorney/administrator? ☐ Yes ☐ No

How could this publication be improved? What else would you like to see in it?

_____

_____

_____

Do you have other comments or suggestions? _____

_____

_____

Name _____

Firm/Company _____

Address _____

City/State/Zip _____

Phone _____

Firm Size: _____ Area of specialization: _____

We appreciate your time and help.

Fold

NO POSTAGE
NECESSARY
IF MAILED
IN THE
UNITED STATES

BUSINESS REPLY MAIL
FIRST CLASS   PERMIT NO. 16471   CHICAGO, ILLINOIS

POSTAGE WILL BE PAID BY ADDRESSEE

AMERICAN BAR ASSOCIATION
PPM, 8th FLOOR
750 N. LAKE SHORE DRIVE
CHICAGO, ILLINOIS 60611-9851

Fold

AMERICAN BAR ASSOCIATION

Membership Application

 Law Practice Management Section

Access to all these information resources and discounts – for just $3.33 a month!

Membership dues are just $40 a year – just $3.33 a month.
You probably spend more on your general business magazines and newspapers.
But they can't help you succeed in building and managing your practice
like a membership in the ABA Law Practice Management Section.
Make a small investment in success. Join today!

☑ Yes! I want to join the ABA Section of Law Practice Management Section and gain access to information helping me add more clients, retain and expand business with current clients, and run my law practice more efficiently and competitively!

Check the dues that apply to you:
❏ $40 for ABA members   ❏ $5 for ABA Law Student Division members

Choose your method of payment:
❏ Check enclosed (make payable to American Bar Association)
❏ Bill me
❏ Charge to my: ❏ VISA®   ❏ MASTERCARD®   ❏ AMEX®

Card No.: _____ Exp. Date: _____

Signature: _____ Date: _____

ABA I.D.*: _____
(* Please note: Membership in ABA is a prerequisite to enroll in ABA Sections.)

Name: _____

Firm/Organization: _____

Address: _____

City/State/ZIP: _____

Telephone No.: _____ Fax No.: _____

Primary Email Address: _____

Get Ahead. 🏃

AMERICAN BAR ASSOCIATION

 Law Practice Management Section

Save time by Faxing or Phoning!
▶ Fax your application to: (312) 988-5820
▶ Join by phone if using a credit card: (800) 285-2221 (ABA1)
▶ Email us for more information at: lpm@abanet.org
▶ Check us out on the Internet: http://www.abanet.org/lpm

750 N. LAKE SHORE DRIVE
CHICAGO, IL 60611
PHONE: (312) 988-5619
FAX: (312) 988-5820
Email: lpm@abanet.org

I understand that Section dues include a $24 basic subscription to Law Practice Management; this subscription charge is not deductible from the dues and additional subscriptions are not available at this rate. Membership dues in the American Bar Association are not deductible as charitable contributions for income tax purposes. However, such dues may be deductible as a business expense.

YES Enroll me in the Section of Real Property, Probate and Trust Law of the ABA for:

$40.00 for regular and associate members

$5.00 for Law Students *(must be an ABA member).*

$15.00 "First Year" for Young Lawyer Division members *(1 year only).*

ABA Member ID

Name

Firm/Organization

Business Address

Business Phone   Fax Number

E-mail Address

Payment Enclosed
(Checks payable to American Bar Association)

Charge my

❑ Visa   ❑ Master Card   ❑ AMEX

Account Number   Exp. Date

Signature

Send me an informational packet on the Section of Real Property, Probate and Trust Law.

Membership in the ABA is a prerequisite to enrollment in the Section.